JO

JONNY

The unofficial and unauthorised biography of
JONNY WILKINSON
by Duane Harewood

Published by
Kandour Ltd
1-3 Colebrook Place
London N1 8HZ

This edition printed in 2004 for
Bookmart Limited
Registered Number 2372865
Trading as Bookmart Ltd
Blaby Road
Wigston
Leicester LE18 4SE

First published June 2004

ISBN 1–904756–04–2

Production services:
Metro Media Ltd

Author: Duane Harewood

Dedicated to Philip Nathaniel Harewood

With thanks to: Jenny Ross, Emma Hayley,
Lee Coventry, Belinda Weber

Cover design: Mike Lomax
Cover Image: Rex Features

Inside Images: Rex Features

© Kandour Ltd

Printed and bound by Nørhaven Paperback, Denmark

FOREWORD

This series of biographies is a celebration of celebrity. It features some of the world's greatest modern-day icons including movie stars, soap personalities, pop idols, comedians and sporting heroes. Each biography examines their struggles, their family background, their rise to stardom and in some cases their struggle to stay there. The books aim to shed some light on what makes a star. Why do some people succeed when others fail?

Written in a light-hearted and lively way, and coupled with the most up-to-date details on the world's favourite heroes and heroines, this series is an entertaining read for anyone interested in the world of celebrity. Discover all about their career highlights – what was the defining moment to propel them into superstardom? No story about fame is without its ups and downs. We reveal the emotional rollercoaster ride that many of these stars have been on to stay at the top. Read all about your most adored personalities in these riveting books.

JONNY WILKINSON

CONTENTS

JONNY WILKINSON

FACT FILE

Full name: Jonathan Peter Wilkinson
Eye colour: Blue
Date of birth: 25 May 1979
Place of birth: Frimley, Surrey, England
Height: 5' 10"
Relationship: Current girlfriend,
Diana Stewart, actress.
Mother: Philippa
Father: Phil
Brother: Mark, whose nickname is Sparks

Star sign: Gemini (20 May–20 June)
Geminis easily become bored and they love to be entertained. They have excellent communication skills and love to listen to gossip. Geminis are great charmers and can be very romantic. One of their biggest problems is that their mouth cannot always keep up with the stream of their thoughts. Famous Geminis include Sir Paul McCartney, Marilyn Monroe, J F Kennedy, Venus Williams, Bob Hope and Judy Garland.

JONNY WILKINSON

Chinese birth sign: Goat

These very genuine individuals and their hearts are in the right place. They always try to do the right thing at every occasion. At times they can be over emotional and are well known for preparing for the worst. The majority will do their utmost to avoid any form of confrontation.

Career High: Jonny signed for Newcastle Falcon straight after leaving school. He represented his country for the first time in a match against Ireland in 1998. He has been awarded International Player of the Year 2002, UK Sports Champion of Champions 2002, Rugby Union Writers Club Personality of the Year 2002. He is the youngest rugby player ever to be awarded an MBE in 2002, he was 23-years-old. He drop kicked the winning goal in the final of the rugby world cup 2003. He was awarded the 50th BBC Sports Personality of the Year 2003, Rugby Players Player of the Year 2003, and the OBE for services to rugby 2004.

1

Jon-Boy

JONNY WILKINSON

JON-BOY

A t a children's rugby match an excited spectator shouted from the touchline: "Kick it Jonny, kick it!" It was a Farnham mini-rugby game and the comment which was aimed at a scrawny five-year-old, had come from the boy's father. Even at this age little Jonny Wilkinson was displaying immense potential. Jonny was born on 25 May 1979 in the leafy Surrey suburb of Frimley. Jon-Boy grew up in a very close-knit family with a strong sporting tradition. His father Phil had played rugby as a forward for Somerset and his mother Philippa had captained Hampshire's ladies' squash team. She also enjoyed

JON-BOY

a set or two of tennis. Jonny's older brother (by 17 months), Mark, was a keen rugby player and even his granddad had been a professional footballer in his time. Sport was in the Wilkinson family's blood.

Philip Wilkinson gradually became frustrated with the way his son's team was being guided and after three years had joined forces with another parent, John Fairley. John Fairley, himself a keen player and supporter, played for the Farnham veterans. His son Alistair, who was a bit older than Jonny, also played for mini-rugby in the junior leagues. Both men were passionate about the game, and decided to enroll on rugby courses to train their sons' teams in the way they saw fit. Fairley became Jonny's first coach and was instantly impressed by the young man's overall ability. Phil meanwhile took charge of Alistair's slightly older team. It was during these early years that Jonathan Wilkinson learnt one of rugby's most important lessons. To get anywhere in the sport, you need an appropriate nickname. Hence Jonathan Wilkinson became Jonny Wilko, and his brother Mark became Sparks. This essential lesson would put him in good stead in the years to come.

Even during those fledgling years Jonny's

JON-BOY

natural self and team motivational skills marked him out from the rest. It was not only rugby that excited Jonny, he also played football and tennis socially. However it soon became clear that rugby would be his number one sport. Wilkinson was in effect just sports mad, he was always active and whatever he turned his hand to, he gave 100 per cent.

John Fairley was very much aware that at the heart of things the children had to enjoy playing the sport, if it ever became a chore the team would lose interest and their natural enthusiasm. As the team gradually became better they started to win more and more competitions growing in confidence with every victory.

When Jonny moved to Pierrepont Secondary School in Farnham, his talents really began to shine. It was here that he met student teacher Matt Payne. One lunchtime Payne indulged the youngster in a little kicking contest to see what he could do. After half a dozen shots during which the young whippersnapper soundly defeated Payne, Wilkinson asked his teacher if he wanted to try kicking with his left foot. It was only then that Wilkinson revealed to his beaten teacher that he had been kicking with his weaker right foot. Being

JON-BOY

beaten by a 12-year-old using his wrong foot did nothing to repair Matt Payne's already bashed ego. However the two worked well together and Wilkinson was able to get some specialist one-to-one tuition. Wilkinson's ability to kick with his weaker right foot was demonstrated with deadly effect 12 years later. Wilkinson had deliberately taught himself to be as proficient with his right foot as he was with his left. It was this type of dedication that would pay off in years to come. Phil said that when his son was around 10-years-old, he wrote his goals on a piece of paper. His mini mission statement proclaimed that he intended to be the best and most respected fly half in the world. Jonny's parents never tried to be pushy parents, if anything it was the other way round, but they did encourage and support his sporting interests. Mr and Mrs Wilkinson spent a great deal of time in the car, waiting around to drive Jonny back home after his promised 45-minute kicking practice extended into a 90-minute affair. Undoubtedly Jonny possesses reservoirs of natural talent, but this has always been supplemented by endless hours of training. He is constantly rehearsing for that flash of spontaneity. It was said that Jonny was so enthusiastic about sport that

JON-BOY

the school decided to give him the key to the gym.

Jonny was not only dedicated to sport, he also found time to commit to his studies. The 13-year-old passed the entrance exams for the prestigious Lord Wandsworth College. The co-ed public school nestled in the Hampshire countryside has a good reputation for sporting excellence. The £17,000-a-year school boasts that it "fosters the intellectual, moral and spiritual development of all young people". Wilkinson thrived in this nurturing atmosphere with its small, intimate class sizes.

By this stage Wilkinson had been playing the oval ball game for nearly 10 years, he was practically a veteran. Although in a new environment, his views on rugby remained unchanged. The school day began at 8:15 and on occasions he would turn up an hour early to practice his kicking skills. The teenager was also known to go down to the grounds during the school holidays to perfect his art. One of the things that drives Wilkinson is failure, and the fear of it. Wilkinson's biggest concern has always been his fear of not being well enough prepared and of letting his side down.

In September 1995, when Wilkinson entered the lower sixth, a new sports and chemistry teacher arrived at the school. Steve Bates, or Batesy to his friends, was a member of the London Wasps and the England Rugby team where he played scrum half. He could see Wilkinson's extraordinary talents, which were highlighted by the ordinary skills of the rest of the team. Being part of the game for so long Wilkinson had developed a keen sense of anticipation, he could read the game well. Steve Bates' Wasp teammate was legendary England fly half Rob Andrew. The England fly half had a blistering turn of speed and excellent left foot kicking skills. The Yorkshireman had kicked off a 12-year career in the game with a triple rugby blue at Cambridge University. He was one of the darlings of English rugby during the Will Carling and Rory Underwood era. He was coming to the end of a successful career. English Rugby was going through some severe changes, it was turning from an amateur sport to a professional one. For the first time players didn't have to fit rugby in around their real paying careers. This also paved the way for the game to be taken and played more seriously in this country. No longer just an enjoyable pastime, it was now a credible business as well.

It wasn't long before Bates was enthusing about his new discovery to Rob Andrew. Andrew had been a long-time hero for Wilkinson as a lad. The two men kept an eye on Wilkinson's development. Rob Andrew moved north to play out the remainder of his career and become director of rugby at the Newcastle Falcons. He soon persuaded his friend and colleague Steve Bates to join him as a coach.

Wilkinson had to balance his sporting life with his academic one. He had always been determined to become a rugby player but he needed something to fall back on if injuries or other unforeseen circumstances interfered with his ambition. He studied hard for three A-levels, biology, chemistry and French. Wilkinson's free time was almost non-existent, but he seemed to work well under the added pressure. Wilkinson had also been trying to catch the eye of the England scouts. In 1997 Wilkinson was selected to play for England's under-18 team. This was a dream come true for the teenager as he finally had the chance to don that cherished England jersey. The under-18s played and beat Ireland, Scotland, France and Wales. They stamped their dominance and Wilkinson was, at last, able to move his game up a level, gaining experience from the other nations.

After that success Wilkinson was drafted into England's under-21s tour of Australia. The

JONNY WILKINSON

JON-BOY

England team won all the matches in their eight game rout. Wilkinson's left foot was pivotal in the team's success and he was quickly becoming a rising star. When he returned home, he was given more good news. Wilkinson had passed his three A-levels and had been accepted to study for his degree at the University of Durham.

Following his outstanding performances in an England shirt, rugby clubs were also vying for the youngster's services. This was a fantastic position for the 18-year-old to be in, but it also placed him in a dilemma. He talked things over with his family and knew that they would support him no matter what he decided. Rob Andrew was keen to tempt the school-leaver up to the northeast, but Wilkinson already had good offers from clubs closer to home. The offer of a two-year contract and the temptation of working with Rob Andrew, one of his all-time heroes, proved too much. Jonny bit the bullet, packed his bags and headed off to the Tyne.

2

A dream fulfilled

JONNY WILKINSON

A DREAM FULFILLED

I t was a very big move for Jonny. He had led a fairly comfortable, cosseted life with his family around him. Jonny's parents had several meetings with Rob Andrew to establish some ground rules. Philippa wanted to know that he'd be properly looked after, not only on the field but off it as well. Jonny hadn't really had to fend for himself before. Phil and Philippa recall how Jonny rang them from his local supermarket once to ask their advice. He wanted to know if he needed a passport to pay for some food with a cheque. One of the first people to greet Wilkinson was the big-hearted Geordie, Steve Black. Black or Blackie to

A DREAM FULFILLED

his friends and his enemies was appointed the Newcastle Falcons conditioning coach. He ensured the players were fit both physically and mentally for the work ahead. More than just a trainer, he was a friend, a father, a counsellor and a mentor to the team. Wilkinson had only just left school and Black understood what a huge transition it was for him. He could see that Wilkinson was really a young boy a long way from home. Black was always on hand with a pep talk or a gag as and when needed. Steve Black was to become an immensely important force in Wilkinson's life.

Wilkinson didn't get many opportunities to show off his talents when he first arrived at the northern club as Rob Andrew wanted to ease him in gently. As a consequence Wilkinson spent much of his first season as a professional player on the bench. When Wilkinson did get the opportunity to do his thing, he played as an inside centre. At the time Rob Andrew was still playing and was one of the best, if not the best, fly half in the world.

It was during this time that Wilkinson first came across specialist England rugby kicking coach, David Alred. He was the man who had coached Rob Andrew, and he was keen to pass on his magical tips to the new boy. Alred, who played

A DREAM FULFILLED

as a kicker in the US for the NFL, has turned kicking into a science. He felt that the kick was similar to the golf swing – the rhythm, the timing, even the addressing of the ball. He refers to it as an upside-down golf swing. Alred taught Wilkinson to channel his energies into his left foot. David Alred completely deconstructed Wilkinson's style, a style that had served him well for 13 or so years. Wilkinson was left in limbo for a time, he wasn't able to use his old style and he hadn't yet mastered the new style.

Wilkinson's unique style is a culmination of what he learned from Alred and his own natural adaptations. Every aspect of Wilkinson's kick is carefully thought out. Wilkinson finds out what brand of ball will be used in forthcoming tournaments so that he can practise with them. Wilkinson has evolved a specific ritual designed to take the risk element out of kicking, starting with the way he places the ball on the plastic kicking tee used to hold the ball upright. In the old days, players would simply dig a lump out of the pitch with the heel of their boot and place the ball in it. This would invariably infuriate groundsmen up and down the country. Wilkinson likes his boot to make contact with the ball at what he refers to as the

A DREAM FULFILLED

"sweet spot". He will often then pull up a few blades of grass and throw them into the air. This is partly so that he can check the force and direction of the wind and partly just habit. He then takes four steps back and five across to the right. Wilkinson then focuses on the exact spot that his boot should hit the ball and the target he wants the ball to hit. Wilkinson visualises a woman sitting in one of the seats behind the posts, and affectionately refers to her as Doris. He targets her, his aim is so pinpointed that the gap between the two upright sticks appears in his mind to be much larger than it actually is. Wilkinson cradles his hands, this acts as a sort of symbolic shield blocking out the noise of the crowd and helps him focus. Wilkinson invariably knows whether or not a strike will be successful the moment the ball leaves his boot. Kicking success at this level has as much to do with mental attitude as it does technique, Wilkinson's procedure helps him get into the right frame of mind.

Wilkinson was given his first opportunity to shine at his new club in the winter of 1998. Newcastle was drawn in a clash against Exeter, weather conditions that day were not the best but the hungry young player was chomping at the bit

A DREAM FULFILLED

to show his worth. The conditions played havoc with his kicking game, high winds robbed the rising star of three kicks, but he still did enough to make his mark on the match. It was only 12 weeks later that England's head coach Clive Woodward called upon Wilkinson to serve his country in the then Five Nations competition. Just like most of the rugby world at the time, Clive Woodward had been monitoring the progress of the diligent newcomer. The Five Nations tournament, a high spot in the rugby calendar, comprised England, Scotland, Wales, Ireland and France. Its roots can be traced back to the 1880s. The Five Nations became the Six Nations when Italy joined the fold in 2000. If any one team beats all of the others, they are awarded the coveted Grand Slam title.

Wilkinson was called as a substitute for the final game in the tournament, played at Twickenham, the home of English rugby. The men in white were up against the Irish. Wilkinson had been warming up and warming down on the sidelines for most of the match during that Saturday afternoon. Then suddenly with a couple of minutes left on the clock and heading for a certain 35-17 victory, England teammate Mike Catt, or rather Catty went down

A DREAM FULFILLED

injured. Jonny Wilkinson was told to play on the wing, and as he stepped up to take his place on the field, he also stepped into the history books. At nearly 19-years-old, he was to be the youngest player to represent his country for 71 years. That brief moment on 4 April 1998 signalled his England debut and fulfilled the first part of Jonny Wilkinson's long-term dream.

Wilkinson's next outing in an England jersey was just as memorable, but for all the wrong reasons. The England team were scheduled to play the southern hemisphere teams including Australia and New Zealand. Clive Woodward's choice of players was severely reduced as many players had been injured or were exhausted after a recent British Lions tour. The British Lions, now called the British and Irish Lions, is a touring team made up of the cream of English, Scottish, Welsh and Irish players and competes against the southern hemisphere nations. With his limited choices Woodward was left to pick from a pool of inexperienced players, among them Wilkinson who had only got two minutes of senior international rugby under his belt. The youngsters were thoroughly thrashed time after time. England suffered their worst defeat for nearly 130 years against Australia with a final score of 76–0. The expedition went on to be known aptly as the 'Tour of Hell'. It was an unmitigated disaster, Wilkinson came back to England battered, bruised and with his morale at an all-time low. Wilkinson hadn't experienced such a major defeat before. It was to prove a very steep learning curve.

On his return, Wilkinson continued to play with the Falcons and he concentrated on club rugby. Rob Andrew intended to let Wilkinson have more games after the tour and to try him out in his favoured fly half position. Wilkinson was making very good progress and was still very young. One of the things that impressed Rob Andrew was the youngster's determination – he always learned from his mistakes and was always looking to prove and push himself. A lot of sportsmen see training as a means to an end – its sole objective being improved performance in their chosen sport. Wilkinson has always had a more ritualistic attitude to training, but what some people find strange is that he actually enjoys it. The harder the training session, the bigger Wilkinson's sense of achievement and the more he grows in confidence. He believes that the harder one works, the luckier one becomes. Even in his early years as

A DREAM FULFILLED

a professional player, he was anxious not to be pigeon-holed. Being 'just' a spectacular kicker was never going to be enough for him, his hunger for all round ability dictated that he would master all aspects of the modern game.

Wilkinson's experience was gradually growing – he was involved in the 1999 Five Nations campaign, and he put his experiences Down Under behind him and looked forward to this latest challenge. He helped his team to victory over Scotland, his trusty and newly developed left foot secured four goal kicks. He did even better on the kicking front with his next match, as his Irish opponents' luck ran out. A fortnight later saw Wilkinson really get into his stride when the formidable French paid a visit to the English home of rugby. The English team couldn't smash through the French team's defence but managed to tot up a 21–10 victory. That day Wilkinson obtained all of England's points through his poised and well-practised kicking skills. It was the Welsh team that would eventually dash England's Five Nation's Grand Slam hopes. Their unexpected last minute flurry resulted in a 31–32 score line.

1999 also happened to be World Cup year and Wales had the honour of hosting the ceremony.

JONNY WILKINSON

A DREAM FULFILLED

England's first opponents didn't really test them, Italy bowed under the pressure, surrendering to a 67–7 thrashing. Wilkinson scored his first ever try in an England shirt and contributed 30 of his country's points. England's next opponents had no intention of making things easy for them. The All Blacks were awesome and they caused problems for the England pack. England did win by 16–30 however, although a good margin it was a fiercely and closely fought contest. Wilkinson finished the game down-hearted, only managing to get half of his eight attempted kicks to go over the bar. Ultimately England was to be seen off by the South Africans, who slaughtered Clive Woodward's boys 21–44.

3

The long road ahead

THE LONG ROAD AHEAD

The following year, Wilkinson and crew had the Six Nations title in their sights. Still smarting from their last defeat against the English, Ireland was up for revenge. England however had other plans, they had no intention of playing ball. They took the opportunity not only to beat but also humiliate the men from the Emerald Isles. England's record breaking 50–18 win aroused English passions, and gave them confidence for their battle across the Channel with the French. It was not the prettiest of games but England got the result that they needed with a 15–9 victory. Things were going well and were

THE LONG ROAD AHEAD

about to get better especially for Jonny Wilkinson. England's third match saw them pitted against Wales. It proved to be an easy match against the disorganised Welsh cover. A stunning performance by Wilkinson led to him scoring 21 of his team's 46 points. Their next opponents, the Italians, also failed to resist the battle-hardy English stalwarts and ended in a 59–12 result. However, the Scottish finally rained on England's Grand Slam parade. The contest was held at Murrayfield, the home of Scottish rugby. Match day was a particularly overcast, windswept scene that did not bode well for England and they went down 19–13.

Woodward never gave up on his team, even though his defeat in the 1999 World Cup had awakened his critics. Luckily for him he had supporters within rugby union. They gave him the time and money needed to take his team forward. He developed a new philosophy for English rugby. He fought for the best facilities and acquired the best trainers in the business. Woodward was not interested in satisfying demands for short-term victories – he had his eye on the long-term bigger picture. Woodward developed new systems of operation for his players which all centred on the player's discipline. He devised a set of rules to which all players would adhere. All of these laws were written in the black book. The players themselves dictated most of the commandments. Among other pledges they agreed to turn up five minutes early for each meeting and to conduct themselves in a professional manner both on and off the field. In return the players were afforded everything they needed to improve their game. Woodward was determined to create a winning environment.

Although some players were sceptical at first, they all bought into the idea. Especially when Woodward drafted in a specialist eye coach. He knew that vision was an integral part of sporting performance, and his new trainer provided exercises for the players' eyes. He also decided that a specialist trainer would be responsible for every aspect of his team's game. Whether it be a scrummage coach, a kicking coach, a throwing coach or indeed an eye trainer. Anything that the players needed would be provided. Woodward also ensured that high standards were further enhanced by the team's mode of travel. The England team would now always travel first, or at very least, business class, he wanted to instill in his men that they

THE LONG ROAD AHEAD

were the best, they had the best and they must always perform to their best abilities. No one was sure whether his ideas would pay off or not.

Wilkinson built on his experiences during the following season. He had made good progress in both the Falcons and the England team. Having started off as the new boy, he was now a firm fixture on both the domestic and international fronts. He had quickly developed from a naïve teenager to a professional senior, fully able to account for himself, performing at the highest of international levels.

2001 saw England again chancing their arm for Six Nations Grand Slam glory. They started well on 3 February, with a 44–15 mauling of their Welsh opponents. Wilkinson kicked home five goals that day much to the dismay of hopeful Welsh souls. After that the geed-up England team set about annihilating their Italian counterparts. England showed off in front of their Twickenham home crowd, quickly pulling away with a 57-point lead. The Italians lost with a demoralising 80–23 divide. Thirty-five of the points were attributed to Wilkinson's left foot. Next in line were the Scottish. England imposed their supremacy over their opponents with a 43–3 score line. After a break in

THE LONG ROAD AHEAD

proceedings due to an outbreak of foot-and-mouth disease, England went on to establish their dominance. Finally England had reached a turning point – they won the Six Nations title but Ireland denied them the enjoyment of a Grand Slam victory with a 14–20 defeat at Lansdowne Road in October.

This year also saw Wilkinson called into the Lion's den. The British Lions realising Wilkinson's talents, recruited him into their midst. It was a major opportunity for him and one that he relished. It was a chance to prove himself yet again and absorb some much-needed confidence playing against the southern hemisphere nations. It would also be an opportunity for the young fly half to exorcise his demons after the disastrous 1998 tour. When Wilkinson was given the opportunity to show his metal, he did so in spades. He orchestrated tries and set up breaks for his teammates against the Queensland Reds.

However, things were not to remain on a high. During a hard tackle on an Australian winger, Wilkinson sustained a painful injury to his leg. His father Phil, who had flown out to support his son, had a heart-stopping moment when he saw Jonny laid low after the encounter. He thought his son had broken his leg, but

THE LONG ROAD AHEAD

whatever it was Phil knew that Jonny was in a great deal of pain and that his career may even be over. With no fractures discovered the fly half made such a fast resurgence that his teammates dubbed him Lazarus, owing to his almighty recovery. He was up and playing again within a week. He returned home with renewed vigour and an even more insatiable appetite for success.

At Twickenham against the All Blacks, Wilkinson scored one of the most spectacular tries of his or indeed any player's international career. It was a crisp, bright afternoon and everything seemed set for a classic trusty Wilkinson drop goal. However, instead of going for the posts he chipped the ball over the heads of the New Zealand defence, then followed it up with a speedy dash. He caught his own passing kick and touched the ball down on the Kiwi's try line. England went on to win 31–28. It had really been Wilkinson's day. He had successfully taken three penalties, slotted over two conversions, stumped up a drop goal and even managed a try. Wilkinson and crew went on to beat Australia 32–31 in what Wilkinson would later describe as one of the best experiences of his life. Beating the world champions was a huge boost and reinforced the team's self-belief.

JONNY WILKINSON

THE LONG ROAD AHEAD

It was only a matter of time before this "new look, new attitude" southern-hemisphere-beating-team claimed the Grand Slam crown. In the 2003 Six Nations crusade England were favourites – they had made their mark and established themselves as world leaders. The French were the first to take the challenge against Woodward's men in a 25–17 result. In a display of sportsmanlike generosity, the French even praised Woodward's men. Seven days later and Wilkinson strikes again. With devastating, cold-blooded accuracy he helps rack up 26 points ahead of Wales's nine. Little did Jonny Wilkinson know that the next time he pulled on an England shirt it would be as captain. Martin Johnson sustained an injury and Woodward looked to Wilkinson to fill the big guy's boots. It was a life-long dream for Wilkinson and he didn't need to be asked twice. England dismissed their Italian rival's 40–5 although the newly appointed skipper was forced to leave the pitch in the second half following an injury to his shoulder. It was a fantastic experience for the fly half. Although not very vocal, in fact positively shy, in his day-to-day life, he was forced to direct the team and dictate their play. The team respected him and his capabilities,

THE LONG ROAD AHEAD

it proved an excellent opportunity for him to realise how much he was valued.

Wilkinson clocked up a hefty 18 points in England's 40–9 victory against the Scots. The only obstacle in England's way of Grand Slam victory was the Irish. It was a bright but gusty afternoon when the white shirts stood toe-to-toe with their green jerseyed opposition. Wilkinson worked hard that day running around as though his life depended on it. He was rewarded with 15 points which helped his team on the way to an overall 42–6 Six Nations Grand Slam winning title. Wilkinson was also named RBS Man of the Match and sustained a bloody bottom lip in the process. England and Wilkinson were now ready to face anything and anyone that was thrown at them. Ahead lay the definitive goal, the World Cup title. Bring it on.

4

Time out

TIME OUT

The pursuit of rugby excellence accounts for about 98 per cent of Jonny Wilkinson's time. When he's not playing, he's practising and when he's not practising on the pitch, he's training away from it. Perhaps in the weights room, building up his upper body strength to assist with the crunching tackles he makes. Or having treatments by the physios. Wilkinson claims that one of the reasons he practises so much is because he can only relax in the knowledge that he has achieved his best. A planned one-and-a-half hour kicking session can easily turn into a three-hour exercise. Wilkinson is often the solitary

TIME OUT

figure out in the park taking scores of shots at the posts until he's met his exacting standards.

When the fly half does eventually drag himself away from the Falcons' Kingston Park ground, he climbs into his sporty dark Mercedes coupe and heads for home. A Coldplay CD provides the soundtrack for the journey, as he drives through the twisting lanes after a hard day's work. Half an hour later Jonny's pulling up on the circular gravel drive outside his secluded Corbridge mansion. Buried in the rolling Northumberland countryside, Jonny shares this gorgeous period property with his older brother, Mark. The house lies on the edge of a private golf course, and sometimes Jonny takes the opportunity to whack a few balls (golf not the oval type) down the fairway. He is very much aware of his competitive perfectionist streak, so is wary not to become too involved with any sport other than rugby. It is for that reason that he avoids playing conventional rounds, golf is purely a distraction from his first sporting love. Wilkinson's family and friends know that if he did take golf seriously, he would be practising his swing well into the night. The boys also enjoy a game of ping-pong, but trying not to be too competitive can be problematic.

TIME OUT

In addition to their passion for sport, the Wilkinson brothers share an enjoyment of music. An airy room at the top of the minimally furnished manor house contains Mark's drum kit and Jonny's guitar. Mark gave his brother the guitar for Christmas and although he can strum a few tunes, he is not yet threatening Eric Clapton or BB King's mantle. In classic bachelor-pad tradition, the boys also enjoy 'vegging' out downstairs in front of their huge television screen, whilst sinking into their matching black leather armchairs. The comfy luxury chairs electronically massage the aches and pains from a pounding day on the pitch. Pure bliss. Jonny is a film buff and his living room shelves display a wide selection of videos and DVD's. The brothers also enjoy visits to the cinema when the opportunity arises.

With both brothers working for the same club, they understand the importance of not talking 'shop' at home. Mark Wilkinson is 17 months older than Jonny. He started off as a conditioning coach at Falcons, but has since been selected for the team. He occasionally dons the prized number 10 jersey in his brother's absence. Jonny and Mark 'switch off' in their home, where everything is very much geared up to winding down.

JONNY WILKINSON

TIME OUT

The Wilkinson's are a very close family, not only do the two brothers live and work together, but Jonny's dad Phil also acts as his and Mark's personal manager, working from an office in Jonny's house. Mr and Mrs Wilkinson moved from Surrey to the north of England to be near to their sons. Phil Wilkinson also worked as a financial advisor so he's able to give his boys expert money guidance. Their manager dad also tends to the boy's garden occasionally, while mum Philippa often addresses the boys' laundry issues. In his professional capacity Phil works closely with Tim Buttimore, Jonny's agent. They vet the endless calls and emails that request interviews and endorsements. Following England's World Cup victory Jonny's popularity has soared sky high, he has been swamped with offers. With his father acting as his personal manager, Jonny can still focus solely on his game. Nothing is allowed to get in the way of Jonny's rugby. In the past Jonny's father has famously stated that his son finds Christmas Day really interferes with his training regime.

Wilkinson has been turning down offers from all quarters, he is anxious to keep control of his image and not to be associated with products and

TIME OUT

services that he doesn't truly believe in. *Hello* and *OK!* magazines have both reportedly offered him lucrative feature deals that Wilkinson has turned down. "Regardless of sums involved, he has to be true to the person he is," his agent Tim Buttimore explained in an interview. Already a wealthy man, Wilkinson's £250,000 salary from Falcons has enabled him to be true to his sport and not make any damaging or rash long-term decisions. Jonny also writes for *The Times* newspaper, he kept readers up-to-date with the World Cup exploits and the paper also host his official website. Although Wilkinson writes for the national press, he notoriously never reads newspapers.

One of Jonny Wilkinson's major sponsors is Hackett clothing store. Specialising in traditional gentleman's tailoring, they have been involved with the English sports star since 2002. They complement one another's image, it's a perfect partnership with both parties benefiting from the affiliation. Wilkinson is also very aware that he is a role model to youngsters and so is mindful to conduct himself in an appropriate manner. As a result he will not be associated with any organisations he feels do not support the ethics or morals that he himself displays. Hackett also sponsors the English Rugby Team as a whole providing their official match suits. Wilkinson also has commercial deals with Tetley's Beer, Mercedes-Benz, Lloyds TSB, Lucozade and Cartier. Jonny's other big backer is Adidas, he recently featured in an advertisement for the sportswear giant alongside England football captain, David Beckham. In the television commercial the two men trade kicks. Adidas also supply Wilkinson's rugby boots – he favours their 'Predator' line. The boots are made especially for him and are produced with different soles to help him perform in various conditions. It is reported that prior to his achievements in Australia, Wilkinson's sponsorship deals together with his Falcons and £120,000-England salary netted him in excess of £1.5 million per annum. However England's newest hero still has a way to go before he amasses David Beckham's £65 million fortune.

It was during the Adidas advert shoot that Wilkinson and Beckham struck up a strong friendship. Both men share the same work ethos and very much admire one another. Beckham rang Wilkinson in Australia to wish him luck before the final and congratulated him on his performance after it. When asked what he thought about Wilkinson's World Cup triumph he said: "It's great, if someone works at his game and practises hard he deserves everything he gets." Beckham has also advised Wilkinson on how to deal with his new-found celebrity status. The Real Madrid player had an idea of how the 25-year-old's life would change after becoming an 'overnight' sensation. Wilkinson is uncomfortable with his fame, he sees himself as part of a team and does not enjoy being singled out for special praise. In Wilkinson's mind he is just doing his job and nothing has changed.

Wilkinson guards his privacy fiercely and was therefore very upset when earlier this year photos appeared of him and his girlfriend, Diane Stewart, relaxing on a beach in Mauritius. Wilkinson's lawyers wrote to national newspaper editors conveying his displeasure at their breach of privacy.

Diane Stewart, a beautiful, blonde actress and model, met Wilkinson while she was studying at Newcastle University. She is a cousin of Jonny's England teammate Will Greenwood. Among other projects she has landed contracts for Marks & Spencer's Credit Card campaign and a role in a TV drama series called *Family*. The golden couple have been seeing each other for over two years.

TIME OUT

They shun the limelight, not wanting to be labelled as rugby's answer to 'Posh and Becks'. So they were particularly put out by the press intrusion during their holiday. The more the couple avoid publicity, the more the media are interested in their private lives and their increased exclusivity.

Wilkinson has made it clear on several occasions that rugby comes first, last year he limited his media and commercial commitments to just 21 days. Jonny has always had more time for charity requests. Along with other members of the England squad, Wilkinson does more then his fair share of work for worthy causes including children's hospitals and adult-orientated charities. In May, Wilkinson had his hands sculpted in their famous clasped pre-kick stance. The life-sized bronze pieces were sold in aid of Tommy's, a charity that funds research into premature birth, miscarriage and stillbirth. Earlier in the year a piece of the Telstra turf was auctioned on the Ebay website raising over £600 for Great Ormond Street Children's Hospital in London.

The fly half aims to dedicate the next 10 years or so to playing rugby, after which he might allow himself some respite. In the meantime he is clear about where his focus lies, as he explained:

TIME OUT

"I'm a professional rugby player. I love doing that and I love trying to do that. I am trying to be professional about it, it's all about what you do on the pitch." What does the future hold after rugby? Well he'll still be fairly young, handsome, intelligent, dedicated, respected and rich. Whatever Jonny Wilkinson's future holds, it's certainly looking rosy.

5

England expects

ENGLAND EXPECTS

It took the England Team 24 hours to reach Australia, but their journey to the rugby World Cup had started four years earlier. The Australian media couldn't wait for the England squad to arrive; acres of newsprint full of pre-match provocations were proving very popular Down Under. For a change, England were odds-on favourites to win the Championship, something that neither the team nor the Aussies were particularly comfortable with. Being the underdogs always helps to alleviate unwanted pressures. As it was, everybody wanted a piece of the team that was tipped for the top. There was an

ENGLAND EXPECTS

arduous round of interviews for Clive Woodward. But the press really wanted to chat with England's not-so-secret weapon, Wilkinson. The relentless enquiries became overwhelming and Woodward soon decided it would be in the teams' best interests if all requests for a Wilkinson interview were declined. This lack of co-operation did nothing to help the team bond with the Australian press. But in an effort to keep the players focused, and their schedules adhered to, bloody-mindedness had to be the order of the day.

The *Sydney Daily Telegraph* responded by printing a voodoo doll image of Wilkinson, for their readers to cut out. Wilkinson and his teammates tried to block out these distractions, trying to focus on the games ahead instead.

England's first match in their two-month-long campaign was with Georgia. It was the first time this country had entered the Championship and their expectations were not high. England resoundingly thrashed the new boys 84–6. More of an exhibition match than a contest, Woodward's men used the experience as a serious training session, avoiding risks and unnecessary injuries.

If the match against Georgia was a stroll in the park for England, their next opponents would prove to be anything but – South Africa, holders of the 1995 title, having beaten the All Blacks 15–12 in a hard-fought game. Historically an excellent rugby nation, South Africa was optimistic. President Thabo Mbeki held a grand reception for the squad prior to their departure where he proclaimed, "I am quite certain the team will do us proud," so no pressure then, eh lads.

The teams clashed on 18 October 2003, in front of a 38,000-strong crowd that included Prince Harry. His Royal Highness was spending a gap year on an Australian ranch, and as a keen rugby supporter, was closely following the team's exploits. At the matches the prince sported the England rugby shirt which Wilkinson had given him. One of the England team's sponsors O_2 (formerly called BT Cellnet) tried to get the prince to scrap his old BT Cellnet shirt and sent HRH their newly branded O_2 tops. However the prince refused to ditch his old style 'lucky' England jersey much to the disappointment of the company.

Widely anticipated that it would be a bruising contest, the match lived up to expectations. The 'bad guys', as Woodward referred to them, attacked ferociously. They were gunning for Wilkinson, he was at the centre of their unwanted attentions. For

ENGLAND EXPECTS

their part the England team had the Springbok's scrum half Van Der Westhuizen firmly in their sights. Woodward figured that Westhuizen was the biggest threat and that by neutralising him early in the game, England would be in with a chance. Springbok star Louis Koen was having a bad day; he didn't take the opportunity of securing much needed points, missing four kicks. In contrast, Wilkinson was on blinding form, during the game he kicked 20 points. Centre, Will Greenwood chased a charged down kick to score the only England try, a delighted Prince Harry jumped to his feet and shared a celebratory embrace with Jayne Woodward, Clive's wife. The 25–6 victory that England won meant that they would not have to face the awesome All Blacks. That try 63 minutes into the game was especially important to Greenwood. Sadly, Greenwood had to return home prematurely for personal reasons. His parting words to the team were: "Don't come back without the William Webb Ellis Trophy."

Wilkinson's significant role in South Africa's defeat did not go unnoticed. The Australian press accused the England team of being too reliant on Wilkinson's left boot. Radio chat shows discussed the frailty of the England team and dismissed their

ENGLAND EXPECTS

victories as unconvincing. England's golden boy, proved an all too obvious target. Their criticisms fell on deaf ears. Unbeknown to them, the biggest critic of Wilkinson's work is Wilkinson himself.

The next test for England's capabilities came in the form of Samoa. The men from the small South Pacific Island gave Woodward's squad the fright of their lives. The carefully rehearsed routines, and set plays that England employed were not paying off. The Samoans ripped the English defence to shreds, after eight minutes of play the team were 10 points down. Nothing seemed to be going right and the team was in disarray. The usually reliable Wilkinson missed an easy kick. This was definitely not the time for Wilkinson to display his 'human' side. The team's morale was low and they had to dig deep for inner resolve. Phil Vickery saved the day with a try five minutes before full-time. Understandably the Aussie media really went to town relishing England's discomfort, they took Pommy-bashing to a new all-time high. England's performance had been far from world class and it was beginning to look as though the team were too dependent on one man.

During the Samoa match Tindall received an

ENGLAND EXPECTS

injury, and Dan Luger was sent on temporarily as a blood replacement. No player is allowed to remain on the pitch if he receives an injury that causes blood loss. The player is temporarily substituted while he receives treatment. His replacement is referred to as a blood replacement. In a mix-up, Tindall returned to the fray while Luger was still on the pitch. For 34 seconds, England had 16 men on the field. This was a serious infringement of the rules. The team was faced with the possibility of having points taken away from them, forcing them to square up to New Zealand. Whatever happened, they would be punished, and the mistake could cost them the World Cup. Clive Woodward was hauled in front of the International Rugby Board Court, the England coach admitted that it was one of the most nerve-racking moments of his life. Albeit unintentionally, England had cheated, and this was a serious crime. Richard Smith QC, the specialist counsel to the England Rugby Team, was one of the squads 22-strong support staff. A keen sportsman himself, Smith's area of expertise was "disciplinary and regulatory work with regard to sporting matters". With Smith fighting his corner, Woodward walked away with a

ENGLAND EXPECTS

£10,000 fine.

Relieved by the outcome, the players were able to relax a little bit before meeting Uruguay. The team took some time out at the Warner Bros' Wet n' Wild Water World theme park on Brisbane's Gold Coast. It proved a welcome diversion and a chance for the world-class athletes to recharge their batteries. Morale was high; there were no real concerns about the South Americans. Woodward decided to leave Wilkinson out of the squad, giving him a rest before the impending big match against Wales. Wilkinson's next match would earn him his 50th cap. Predictably England trounced their Uruguayan opponents, but what couldn't have been foreseen was their monumental 111-13 score line. Uruguay was philosophical in defeat, describing the experience as an important learning curve in their development. Spirits and camaraderie were high.

The 100 per cent win record that the team had enjoyed was about to be challenged yet again. The success that Welsh Rugby had enjoyed during the Seventies was a dim and distant memory – the dragons had lost their fire. Even the memorable victory that the team enjoyed against England in 1999 was beginning to fade. However, Wales were

ENGLAND EXPECTS

starting to fight back, rebuilding their side and their reputation. As the underdogs they had nothing to lose, unlike the English team.

The game didn't start well for the boys in white. The Welsh backs ran rings around England, making them look amateur and severely unprepared against their opponents' onslaught. Everything seemed to be going against the favourites, the team were making basic handling errors. Luger sliced a kick in his own half while 10–3 down. It was a total nightmare. The half-time whistle came as a welcome relief. The English players entered their changing room with their heads hung low. They were tired and disheartened. They needed to take drastic action.

One of the rules of the team was that they didn't talk for the first three minutes upon entering the changing room. They used that time to change their shirts prepare for the second half and wait for Clive Woodward to administer his measured pep talk.

Not this time. Captain Johnson, exasperated by his and his teammates' efforts, quite simply exploded. Unleashing "both barrels", Johnson was not about to give up on his dream. They had 40 minutes to turn things around, but if they were going to lose, they were going to go down fighting. Johnson's impassioned rant peppered with "one or two" traditional Anglo-Saxon terms did the trick. Woodward had nothing to add. The coach did make one change, he replaced Dan Luger with Mike Catt. That day Catt contributed a fresh pair of legs and a new energy into the team. A newly invigorated Jason Robinson covered ground, making a darting run deep into the Welsh half, dancing around five Welsh players before off-loading the ball for a Greenwood try. Wilkinson also seemed revived, and helped take the team to a 29–17 victory. The score line belittled the Welsh team's efforts and didn't win England any new friends. Woodward was fully aware that if his players didn't raise their game, they didn't stand a chance against the French.

In the team talk during the post-match analysis Woodward singled Wilkinson's performance out for particular praise. He knew that the pressure was on his young number 10. Wilkinson hadn't had a good game and he needed a boost. He knew that the Aussie media were ripe to tear him apart. Normally Woodward didn't pull his punches but he was a big believer in the game of psychology and used it. He didn't take that attitude with others though, he slated their performances. The squad watched a videotape of their performance, and every aspect of game was analysed for better or worse. The squad was left in no doubt as to what was needed.

France, in public, didn't have any time for the English team. Their bravado felt that they had nothing to worry about, the French were stylish, they had flare and a certain vra vra vroom, whatever that really means. The Australian press praised the chic Gallic boys' imaginative play and damned the Englishmen's boring functionality. At least the weather was on England's side – it was bucketing down with strong winds, classic English rugby weather. The English fans were in good voice that night – the hardcore barmy army had been swelling in numbers as England progressed through the tournament. Support back home was also getting stronger as even non-rugby fans became aware of a little competition with a strangely shaped ball that was being conducted on the other side of the world.

French winger Aurélien Rougerie knocked the ball on giving England a scrum that set Wilkinson up for his first three points. Nine minutes into the game the fly half had already stamped his mark, scoring with his 'wrong' right foot. The French replied one minute later as flanker Serge Betsen piled through the white shirt defence to secure a try. Betsen's

ENGLAND EXPECTS

triumph was diminished later on, when he put a late tackle into Wilkinson, gaining the flanker a yellow card for his effort and sending him off to the sin bin. Any player 'awarded' the yellow card must sit in the 'sin bin' for 10 minutes giving the opposition an advantage. The yellow card is given to any player who seriously infringes the rules. Betsen's actions were to punish his team, allowing Wilkinson to hit a penalty. Wilkinson's kicking game further improved with under half an hour to go. Wilkinson kicked five penalties and chipped three drop goals totting up 24 points to France's seven.

When Paddy O'Brien blew the final whistle England were through to the World Cup Final. The team were on the verge of their biggest match ever. The fact that Wilkinson had been responsible for all of England's points further endorsed his sporting superstar status. It hadn't been a beautiful display but it got the job done. The wet conditions and resulting greasy ball dictated that handling would be difficult, it was always going to be a kicker's game. The match also produced a new world record for prop Jason Leonard. He was brought on two minutes before full time to gain his 112th English cap. France's Philippe Sellas had held the previous record with 111 caps for his country.

6

The final

THE FINAL

So the game was on. England was set to play Australia, the current rugby world champions, on their home turf. It was to be a truly daunting task. The entire Australian nation had been behind their boys from day one. Rugby support in the UK had never matched that of their antipodean cousins. However a groundswell of support was beginning to emerge. The team went into a lock down mode, all of their attention was focused on the big match ahead. They seemed oblivious to other distractions. Clive Woodward was faced with the privilege of selecting his World Cup dream team. Like most managers, Woodward had played 'pick your fantasy

THE FINAL

team' many times before. The 30-man squad had also all dreamed of being part of the final 15-man World Cup squad. Thanks to hard work from Woodward's back room staff – the physios, trainers and medical staff – all of the men were fit for selection.

When the day for the big announcement came, Woodward gathered the team together to break the news to them. He unveiled his team, the chosen players felt elated as they had reached the pinnacle of their careers. The seven reserves knew that they were in with a chance. However it was the eight men who knew that they hadn't got a chance of playing in the World Cup that Woodward had most admiration for. Although they knew that their tour was over, they still trained as hard as ever, never letting their heads drop, never betraying how they truly felt to have their dreams shattered.

The team were determined to treat this game just like any other, the 48th match of the tournament. Their routine didn't change. The barmy army gave the team a good send-off from their hotel. Dressed casually in their tracksuits, the squad looked relaxed when they arrived at the stadium. The team sorted out the formalities before starting a leisurely warm-up. Wilkinson put in one hour's worth of kicking practice with

THE FINAL

Alred. Conditions were far from ideal although the rain possibly marginally favoured England, mirroring many Twickenham matches.

The captains led their respective teams out behind flag bearers. Each team trailed past the William Webb Ellis trophy that was on display near the tunnel exit. It gave them a reminder if one were needed, of what they were there for. The World Cup Championship is a relatively new event in the rugby calendar. It was only established 16 years ago, that's no time at all for a sport that has been in existence for nearly 200 years. New Zealand's All Blacks were the first to lift the trophy. Four years on, in 1991, it was the Australians who laid claim to it. South Africa won the glorious World Cup title under the watchful eye of a jubilant Nelson Mandela in 1995 then four years on, it was returned to the Wallabies.

England skipper Martin Johnson got his men into a huddle for a final pep talk before both teams lined up for the national anthems. The England Team belted out a passionate rendition of *God Save the Queen*. Emotions were running high. Some of the players knew that this would probably be their last match for their country. They had reached their peak both physically and

THE FINAL

mentally. They were glad of the opportunity to bow out at the top of their careers. At last the time had come, the ceremony and the talk was now over, it had taken four years for Woodward's men to reach this point. It was time for the hype to stop and the game to begin.

Andre Watson, the South African referee, blows his whistle. Wilkinson kicks off, and it's game on. Jason Robinson is the first English player to get his hands on the ball, a screen of Australian yellow jerseys immediately surrounds him. The ball comes to Dallaglio but his pass goes astray, Wilkinson temporarily rescues a potentially tricky situation by nudging the loose ball into touch. This prompts the first lineout of the game. Australia throw the ball in, win the lineout and then run at the English defence. The Wallabies drive forward. As England drag one man down there's another Australian player to take his place. When the Australians run out of space on one side of the pitch, they simply move the ball to the other side and resume the onslaught. Finally an Australian mistake gives England the scrum. The boys in white win the ball and Wilkinson boots it safely into touch.

The Australians seem very much in control as they test the England defence searching for

THE FINAL

weaknesses. Martin Johnson leaps and wins the ball from a lineout, and at last England retain some control over the proceedings. The ball is passed out to Martin Tindall. Trapped in his own half, the centre is faced with few options other than kicking it into touch. It soon becomes apparent that with the greasy ball disrupting handling and slippery conditions under foot, kicking skills will be crucial. Australia is awarded a penalty after Watson spots prop Trevor Woodman throw what looks like a punch. The Aussies kick the ball deep into the England's half, piling on the pressure. Somewhat flustered Woodward's men make a mistake – they have too many men in the lineout. It's Australia's throw-in so they dictate the number of men in the line and England is penalised. Australia put the ball into the scrum and retain it until their fly half Steven Larkham is in position. The ball is passed to him and he punts a beautifully weighted kick towards the English corner flag, his backs chase it as it sails along. Australian winger Lote Tuqiri beats Jason Robinson using his seven-inch height advantage to full effect as he out-jumps the England player. Tuqiri lands with the ball safely in his hands over the England try line. The

THE FINAL

Australian fans erupt as the English fans fall silent. Six minutes played, five points gained. This was not the start England or their fans wanted. Elton Flately failed to convert the try being denied by the nearside post.

Wilkinson kicks to restart the game. England attempt to set up another attack, scrum half Matt Dawson starts off a chain, feeding the ball out to Wilkinson who throws to centre Will Greenwood, who then passes on to full back Josh Lewsey. However, the momentum is lost when a crunching Australian tackle hammers into Lewsey. Somehow England keep possession and Robinson is given the ball, but sadly not the space. The Australians, aware of his lightning turn of speed, close down on him, and with no room to manoeuvre he passes the ball on. England spread themselves wide across the pitch, reviewing their options, trying to find holes in the tight Aussie defence. As soon as an English shirt has possession of the ball, yellow jerseys swamp him. The English players try to slow down the pace of the game in an effort to regroup themselves and gather their thoughts. England isn't gaining any ground. The flowing artistry that they displayed in previous confrontations seemed to have eluded

THE FINAL

them. Woodward looked concerned, but the team kept their heads up. The English, although covering no ground, remain in control of the ball. A frustrated Australia commits an error and a penalty is awarded to England. There's only one man on everybody's mind, and Wilkinson steps up to take care of business. It's not a difficult angle but it's a long way from the upright posts. Wilkinson whacks it over and secures three points. The English fans are reawakened, as Wilkinson racks up his 100th point of the championship.

England winger Ben Cohen makes an excellent catch from the Australian restart kick before being brought down by a fearsome Wallaby attack. Wilkinson's left foot is again called upon to sort out the situation. It doesn't fail him, he blasts the ball 55 metres down the field and into the safety of the touchline. The pressure eased off England, and for the moment they have some breathing space. It's Australia's throw-in, they win the ball and come at England with renewed vigour. Wilkinson is forced to make a potentially try-saving tackle as an opponent slips through the defence line. He doesn't floor him but just slows him up enough. When the Australian centre is injured, it gives both teams the chance of a

THE FINAL

breather while he receives treatment. The game has been played at a frantic pace. When play resumes, flanker Neil Back with the ball tucked firmly under his arm, sees a gap and sprints for it but is brought down by a solid wall of Australian shirts. As always Dawson is on hand to tidy things up and re-launch the attack with his backs. Greenwood passes out to Robinson who in turn finds Cohen, but the England pace man has nowhere to run as Aussie jerseys shadow his every move.

Woodman and Dallaglio take matters into their own hands driving forward a few meters into Australian territory. England are desperate to retain possession but don't cover much ground. Australia is frustrated and make an error. They won the ball but knocked it on in the process. England are awarded a scrum, the Telstra barmy army find their voices again. Shouts of England! England! reverberate around the Olympic stadium. Dawson gathers the ball from the scrum and makes a bolt for it, supported by Dallaglio. At last England seem to be making a break for it and are moving forward. Aussie full back Larkham tackles Cohen but he didn't have the ball. Larkham concedes a penalty against his team and a serious cut to his face. He is 'blood-binned'

THE FINAL

and goes off to get stitched up. Meanwhile England's number 10 prepares to add insult to his opposite number's injury by totting up another three points. England is in the lead for the first time.

After the restart Australia recover the initiative and the ball. Larkham's blood replacement Stirling Mortlock runs at the English defensive line. Wilkinson makes a point of seeking him out, he hits him hard lifting him into the air and dumping his unceremoniously on his back. It was more than just a tackle, it was a public statement of strength. The Australian loses the ball in the tackle. A few minutes later Dawson sets Wilkinson up for a drop goal attempt, and the Australians are relieved when the fly half kicks it wide of the posts. Twenty-four minutes into the match and Wilkinson throws himself at Australia's Stirling Mortlock again with his usual aggressive determination. Wilkinson's right shoulder is injured so he stays down. His teammates are on the rampage, lock Ben Kay is within spitting distance of scoring a try, but he knocks the ball on. The England fans hold their heads in despair – it is the closest the team have come to scoring a try in nearly half an hour of play. With the excitement subsiding, all eyes fall

THE FINAL

on the slain Wilkinson. His shoulder took a heavy blow along with English hearts. A trainer attends to him and soon he's back in the fray, his adrenaline and the occasion helping to block out the pain. It's a good thing too because moments later he is called upon to do what he does best. England are awarded a penalty, Wilkinson turns it into three points with his usual professional ease. A few minutes later, following a ruck, Dawson passes the ball out to Dallaglio, who runs at the Australian line and is finally brought down, but not before taking two yellow shirts down with him. Before hitting the ground Dallaglio throws a well-timed pass to the ever-present Wilkinson. The feisty fly half draws two Wallabies into him before offloading the ball to Robinson. With two Australian players in pursuit Robinson dashes for the line, heading for the corner flag. The 5' 8" pocket-rocket slides across the line and scores England's first try. Jumping up he yells, "Come on!", and punches the ball into the air. He's totally pumped up, along with the crowd. Bars, pubs and living rooms across Australia and England erupt in spontaneous cheers. Although Wilkinson fails to convert the try, England and their supporters are really fired up. Australians are relieved when Watson blows the half-time whistle.

7

Under pressure

UNDER PRESSURE

Australia kicks off the second half, with enthusiasm and revitalised energy. Johnson leads the charge attempting to crash through the Wallabies wall, but when his advance is halted there's another England shirt vying for the ball. As each man lines up to test the Aussie resolve, the hardy Australians answer all of their questions time and again. The gold shirts are given some respite, kicking the ball into touch. The Australians have the throw in, but their aerial acrobatics fail to secure the ball, and England win possession again. The players are further encouraged by a stirring verse of *Swing*

JONNY WILKINSON

UNDER PRESSURE

Low Sweet Chariot coming from the stands.
Tindall gets a pass from Wilkinson and fires the
ball down the field into the Aussie half and they
are in retreat. England can virtually smell the
opposition goal line. The home nation must slow
things down, and a well-placed punt finds touch
and takes the heat off a bit. Australian morale is
lifted and they see a chance to turn things
around. A succession of skillful moves gets them
to within 23 metres of the visitor's line. England
put in a long throw right to the back of the
lineout, but the tactic doesn't pay off and
Australia rush to gain possession. Dallaglio goes
offside and presents Elton Flately with an easy
three-point penalty kick.

The score line is now 14–8, Australia are
catching up – they are still very much
contenders. England can't afford to relax or give
away any more penalties. Buoyed up by recent
success the Wallabies keep up the pressure, and
their tenacity is repaid with a Phil Vickery
infringement that results in another penalty.
Flately relishes the opportunity and his
precision boot closes the gap 14–11. It is
becoming a tremendously hard-fought battle
with so much at stake, the forwards, usually

UNDER PRESSURE

such amicable fellows, are winding up their opposite numbers. There is no love lost between them. When the referee intervenes it's a brave man that stands between the two packs weighing over 277 stone. (Aussie pack weigh 1922lbs England pack 1962lbs in total.)

Will Greenwood, England's number 13 misses a tackle, but Wilkinson acting like the predator he is, drags the golden jersey down like a lion with its prey. But things are not going to plan – England is caught on its back foot and is in disarray. With Australia dictating the play, the northern hemisphere combatants are left floundering in their wake. They are moving the ball around with almost balletic elegance, giving the visitors an unwanted masterclass in textbook rugby football.

At a lineout the England team fight back gaining the upper hand. Their combined experience and relentless training are starting to pay dividends. They act upon Clive Woodward's favourite buzzwords, 'T-CUP' – taking control under pressure. With 10 minutes to go in the game, it's the Aussies turn to feel the pressure. Wilkinson makes a darting run into the Aussie half, probing the defence, testing their stamina,

UNDER PRESSURE

their agility and their hunger. He passes to Lewsey who has accelerated up behind him. When he's grounded, Dawson mucks in laying the ball out to Wilkinson again, then Vickery. Dawson's assessing the options – Wilkinson is in position, he's in range for a shot. An attempted drop kick is definitely on the cards. Dawson throws a long pass back to the fly half. He takes a pop with his favoured left foot, but the ball floats wide. The despair on Clive Woodward's face is mirrored by the English fans.

It's now three minutes from full time and both teams are tired. Mike Tindall has cramp and is replaced by Mike Catt. Both parties have made a few silly mistakes. England haven't capitalised on all the opportunities they were given. The Australians know that the Webb Ellis Trophy is slipping away from their grip, it's a prize they believe is rightfully theirs. They are not about to give up now. They dig deep into their reserves for a final push. Their determination is rewarded when they win a scrum a few metre's shy of the England line. Then disaster strikes for England. The referee accuses the front row of deliberately collapsing the scrum and awards a penalty. Flately is given the chance to level the score and become a national

UNDER PRESSURE

hero. He sets up the ball for what could be the most important kick in his career. A consummate professional, he remains totally calm and executes his duty, saving the day for his countrymen. Watson blows the full-time whistle.

When captain Martin Johnson gathers his team around him on the field, the volume of noise in the stadium is such that the boys can barely hear what he's saying. He tells his men to remain focused, not to dwell on the past 80 minutes but to look forward. Clive Woodward doesn't need to address his players, he knows what Johnson will be saying and has nothing new to add. Instead Woodward goes in search of fly half Wilkinson to make sure that he's happy and pass on some suggestions. However, Wilkinson is not in the mood for a chat, almost dismissing Woodward he runs off to practise his kicking. His actions completely astonish the head coach. They were in the middle of the World Cup final and his star player wants to squeeze in a practice kicking! Woodward was beginning to question his star player's sanity.

But Wilkinson just needed to reassure himself, he had to know in himself that he was up to the task in hand. He wanted to be sure that if,

UNDER PRESSURE

or when, he was called upon, he would deliver the goods. This last minute training session was more psychological than practical. Wilkinson relaxes when he's practising his kicking, this one last effort helped him to remain composed and block out the enormous pressures. Wilkinson was happy even though Woodward was bewildered.

*Jonny Wilkinson proudly showing off the William Webb Ellis
trophy following England's victory over Australia in the
World Cup Championship in November 2003.*

THAT kick!

Jonny Wilkinson is not only a hit on the field, but with his boyish good looks he has proved to be a hit off the field too.

In recognition of his cracking year, Jonny Wilkinson was voted BBC's Sports Personality of the Year, 2003.

8

That kick!

JONNY WILKINSON

THAT KICK!

T he England supporters, having recovered from the nail-biting final seconds, have found their voice again. *Swing Low Sweet Chariot* heralds the start of extra time. The teams are faced with 10 minutes each way. Jason Leonard joins the field as England's most capped player with 112 appearances under his belt. The prop brings 14 years of experience with him when he runs on that evening. Within one minute of play England is given the chance they need with an awarded penalty. Australians jeer as Wilkinson steps up to start his familiar routine. He blocks out the shouts both positive and negative. The posts

THAT KICK!

are a good 50 metres away from him, that's right at the top end of his range. So totally focused, Wilkinson can't even hear the crowd. He looks calm on the surface, but underneath his heart is pounding away and he can feel it. He gives the ball a serious whack. The ball's trajectory is straight and true, but the length is in question. The ball begins to dip before it reaches the cross bar. It just manages to clear, it's an excruciatingly tortuous experience for England fans and players alike.

Back home in the UK some 15,000 bars and rugby clubs have applied for early morning liquor licenses, but their customers are finding the on-going proceedings difficult to stomach. However, whilst the nation was glued to their television sets, Philippa Wilkinson was busy shopping in her local branch of Tesco's. She hadn't forgotten the match was on nor was she in desperate need of a pint of milk. Jonny's mother couldn't bear to watch her son's big game. Even the thought of it made her nervous. It was probably a good thing that she wasn't watching that day, because she would have had kittens for sure.

England had reclaimed the lead 17–14, but no one doubted a fierce and robust Australian retaliation. Mike Catt with his fresh pair of legs

THAT KICK!

sets off on a blistering sprint leaving the Wallabies to snap at his heels, England veteran Dallaglio backs him up. The two men power onwards. When their way is blocked, the omnipresent Dawson swoops in to set the ball up again. The two sides gain and lose possession and territory with neither team able to gain total control. Mike Catt tries a drop goal but with no success, then shortly before half time Wilkinson has a bash, but he doesn't hit the target either.

Watson signals half-time and the players are given a five-minute break in which to change ends and get watered. The players are visibly tired, their muscles aching from this epic gladiatorial contest. Old injuries begin to resurface, Johnson motivates his team, and Woodward looks on. He trusts his captain's judgment implicitly. The players are chomping at the bit to get on with the game. Both teams are ready and waiting to go after only two and a half minutes of their break. The referee's whistle to start the game comes as a welcome relief. With 10 minutes left on the clock the game plans are simple, the Australians are desperate to score, and the English are desperate to stop them. During a break in play Moody comes on in place of a cramp-ridden Richard Hill. Five

THAT KICK!

minutes into the last half, Robinson is tested to the limit, he has to bring down his nemesis Tuqiri with a try-saving tackle. The ball goes into touch and the Australians have the throw-in and win the ball. Gold shirts are queuing up to take the ball to the England try line that by now is a mere 12 metres away. The Australians are constantly chipping away at the English defence searching for any chinks in their armour. Finally Australia is given a penalty for a breech by the England skipper. With an estimated 3 million people watching him on television around the world, Flately lines up the place kick, and the Wallaby crowd screams their relieved delight as the ball sails through the uprights.

There are two minutes left, the score is 17 a piece and the tension is tangible. The teams are faced with the prospect of a 10-minute sudden death session if they can't settle the score. Emotions are running high in this rollercoaster ride of a game, time is running out and something's got to give. The spectators, never mind the players, couldn't take much more of this excitement. Suddenly there's a tiny gap in the Australian defence and white shirts pile through. Scrum half Dawson waits patiently at the edge of

THAT KICK!

the tangled bodies ready to make a move. Wilkinson is in position, he's expecting a pass from Dawson. The Australians were assessing the threat – they too expected the ball to find Wilkinson, even Dawson was expecting to pass out to Wilkinson. Therefore it was no wonder that everyone was wrong-footed when Dawson suddenly took it upon himself to make a last minute dash for the line. As a result he gained 20 valuable metres, getting Wilkinson closer to the posts. However now there's a problem. Dawson is trapped beneath a bundle of gold shirts. It's essential that the world-class scrum half is free to make that crucial pass to Wilkinson, nothing can be left to chance. Johnson spotting the dilemma comes up in support. He is given the ball and drives hard into the formidable Wallaby wall. This gives Dawson time to get to his feet and back into position. Everyone knows what England will attempt to do and which man will be called upon to do it. The time has come for Wilkinson's ultimate test. The crowd, Australians and English alike, are on their feet. Dawson plucks up the ball and unleashes a long floating pass back to Wilkinson. It is a routine that the two men have rehearsed many times, there is no time to think as

THAT KICK!

the training takes over. With the tormenting sight of the Australian players scrambling towards him, Jonny Wilkinson carrying his nation's hopes on his shoulders drop kicks for what BBC Radio 5 call "World Cup glory". The minute it leaves his boot Wilkinson knows that he has struck the winning kick. The ball soars high and glides through the posts. In the space of just two seconds, Australia's fate and Jonny Wilkinson's future are simultaneously secured.

In the stadium and back in the UK, fans erupt, the Australians are stunned into silence with their dreams shattered. There was little more then 10 seconds left on the clock. The Australians restart the game, and England win the ball, Dawson passes it out to Catt who in turn blasts it off the field high into the stands. Andre Watson blows for full-time and with that, the England Rugby Team become the champions of the world. Explosive pyrotechnics are set off in Telstra Stadium in celebration of the victory. An ecstatic Wilkinson jumps up and down embracing centre Will Greenwood. Wilkinson is shouting: "World Cup! World Cup!" as if by way of reaffirming the win. As confetti falls from the stadium roof some English players shed tears of joy. Their

THAT KICK!

inconsolable Australian counterparts just feel the pain of loss and 100 minutes of hard fought rugby.

In the post match interview proud captain Martin Johnson pays tribute to their fans, his teammates and the support staff. He also picks out his fly half for added praise, "Wilko was there and right at the death you'd have no one else." Each member of the squad receives a loud cheer as the Australian Prime Minister puts winners' medals around their necks. For most of them the victory has not even begun to sink in. The last person in the line is head coach Clive Woodward. Then comes the moment that England is waiting for, Martin Johnson is presented with rugby's holy grail, the William Webb Ellis Trophy. Johnson lifts the spoils of war above his head, soaking up the atmosphere and adulation with his teammates. The 2003 England Rugby Team are on top of the world. Every one of them, heroes.

9

Rugby football's coming home

RUGBY FOOTBALL'S COMING HOME

T he morning after the night before, some players awoke bleary eyed, not sure whether or not the entire past 24 hours had been a dream. Other players who had been up all night were just returning to their hotel following an on-going 15-hour celebration. It was reported that the local constabulary gave some players a lift back to their five star accommodation. Wilkinson arose on that Sunday morning feeling battered and bruised from the game – he hadn't had a particularly heavy night, but had succumbed to a couple of beers. The traditionally punctual squad were running slightly behind time that morning. Not quite business as usual, but the team still had their formal debriefing. It was not a time for post-match analysis or to discuss the things that could have been improved. England had won, that's all that mattered. Clive Woodward took the opportunity to pay special thanks to his backroom staff, the unsung heroes that kept the England machine rumbling on. Addressing his entire squad Woodward said, "You guys have become a great, great team and you'll never ever forget this...I think that when you get home and look back in days and months to come you'll actually realise how special this is."

Then it was time to face the media. The press pack had just one thing on their mind and that was Wilkinson mania. The questions started in earnest, how did it feel... what was it like... what was going through your mind? "It's indescribable," a somewhat overwhelmed Wilkinson told BBC News crews. Always eager to share the praise, Wilkinson very much emphasised the group's hard work, "I was at the end of a massive team effort". Captain Johnson told BBC News crews that his self-effacing fly half, "is a very special player, a very special person".

The Australian media took the defeat

surprisingly well. "They were well coached, well led...they are the most deserving of champions," relented *The Australian* newspaper. Whilst *The Sydney Morning Herald* admitted, "You played with class, toughness and grace. You were bloody superior." In the UK, *The Daily Mirror* were even more succinct "Champions of the world". The Australian press also resoundingly praised the behaviour of the 50,000 die-hard English fans who had been so vocal in their support.

The 24-hour flight back to England gave the players the opportunity to catch up on some much needed rest and reflect on their victory. During the flight England skipper Martin Johnson and other team members posed for photographs with the cup and signed numerous autographs for passengers and crew.

Meanwhile, back home in Blighty, the British Airport Authority and Metropolitan Police were trying to speculate about the number of fans that might come to greet the players. People started arriving at Heathrow's Terminal Four late on Monday evening hoping to see them returning home. The fans were in good voice, good spirits and there was a party atmosphere. It was a very mixed crowd – men, women, boys and girls came armed with their flags and cameras. The England Team's Boeing 747 renamed 'Sweet Chariot' for the return trip, touched down at approximately 4:35 on a chilly Tuesday morning. An ear-shattering cheer went up from the waiting crowds as the flight's arrival was announced. This prompted yet another chorus of *Swing Low Sweet Chariot*. It was to be another 20 minutes before the team emerged from the plane and was met by Minister for Sport, Richard Caborn MP.

As the boys were led through Passport Control, they had no idea what was about to hit them. Head coach Clive Woodward was the first to finally step out into the Arrivals Hall and was greeted by a barrage of noise. Approximately 10,000 people had assembled to welcome their team home. Nobody had predicted that the English not having won a World Cup for nearly 40 years, would take full advantage of this hard-won victory. The players came out in dribs and drabs – Dallaglio, Greenwood, Hill. The fans swamped Captain Martin Johnson as he loftily brandished the William Webb Ellis Trophy. The crowds, restrained behind crash barriers surged forwards, trying to touch the prize, in what proved to be the hardest scrum of Johnson's 11-

year career. All of the squad were overwhelmed, Wilkinson was one of the last to emerge, surrounded by police, and he received the biggest cheer. As the crowd chanted, "Jonny! Jonny!" he looked visibly shell-shocked as the countless flashguns went off in his face. The police struggled to keep the procession moving and the crowds at bay. A man who was virtually unknown outside the world of rugby had suddenly become the most famous face in Britain. People who had previously had no interest in the oval balled game addressed the sport with new enthusiasm. The impact of the victory was slowly beginning to dawn on the jetlagged team. After battling through the crowds, the players finally boarded the coach and bid farewell to the fans. The squad sat in almost silent bewilderment as police outriders escorted them through the deserted streets of West London and on to their press conference at the Pennyhill Park Hotel in Surrey. When asked by BBC News how he felt about the airport reception Wilkinson claimed, "I am overawed by the support... it's hugely humbling and massively uplifting." Jonny later returned to the tranquillity of his Northumberland retreat hoping to have some time to himself. As he drove up to his house he saw a press pack gathered outside. Wilkinson turned on his heels and made a dash for his parents' home, only to discover that the paparazzi had again taken the initiative and were camping outside. With his sanctuaries overrun with reporters, he headed off to his third home, the Falcons' ground. He wasn't surprised to see the waiting press there, and happily obliged them with yet another news conference. The next morning Wilkinson was more relaxed when he was able to enjoy his first post World Cup training, the 24-year-old felt that a sense of normality was again beginning to return to his chaotic life. How wrong he was.

10

A nation gives thanks

JONNY WILKINSON

A NATION GIVES THANKS

P reparations were quickly made for some form of victory parade to celebrate the new World Champions. The date was set for 8 December 2003 for what was to be the official welcome home – a chance for the public to see the team and join in the celebrations. The Rugby Football Union were not sure how many people would bother to turn out to greet the conquering heroes on a cold Monday lunchtime. Rugby had never really been that popular among the masses and they didn't want the team to be humiliated. The RFU had seriously underestimated rugby and Jonny Wilkinson's new-found popularity.

JONNY WILKINSON

A NATION GIVES THANKS

Seven-hundred-and-fifty-thousand people crammed the streets of central London to show their appreciation. Roads were closed and 500 extra police were drafted in as masses of people made their way to the capital. Westminster Council, concerned that some of the younger rugby fans might be tempted to bunk off school, were moved to issue the statement "The Education Department will be taking a tough line on truancy."

At precisely 12 noon, the Lord Mayor of Westminster, Jan Prendergast, kicked off the parade by cutting a giant red ribbon that was draped across Marble Arch. The players' open-topped bus trundled through, with the legendary Webb Ellis Trophy taking pride of place at the front. One item that hadn't quite made the long-haul flight back from Australia was the 'Gilbert' rugby ball that was used in the winning kick. It had gone missing after the match and was reportedly being held hostage by the Australians. Sydney's *Daily Telegraph* ran a feature entitled "Want the ball? Then give us the Ashes", referring to the fact that the Cricket Ashes remained at Lords even though the Australians had won them. *The Sun* newspaper counter-attacked in the best of tabloid traditions by screaming "Give us our ball back."

JONNY WILKINSON

A NATION GIVES THANKS

Passing underneath Marble Arch is a privilege usually reserved for royalty, and not generally the sporting types. The team, smartly turned out in their light blue shirts, grey suits and brown shoes, looked as excited as the crowds that were waiting to greet them. Many of the team had brought along digital camcorders and cameras to record the historic events. The England rugby team has always had time for their fans, and they have always seemed to be somehow more accessible then the England soccer squad. A second bus with Clive Woodward and his backroom staff closely tailed the players' vehicle, whilst the press pack brought up the rear. They made slow progress down Oxford Street helped by mounted police, as fans packed the pavement, hung out of shop or office windows climbed up scaffolding and even shinned up traffic lights and lampposts to get a better view. The crowd was over 20 deep, made up of tourists, builders, office workers, and even some truanting schoolchildren making a bold appearance. Many of these revellers hadn't watched the game but just wanted to be part of the occasion, to be part of and soak up that feel-good factor. Ticker tape and balloons rained down on the buses as they

A NATION GIVES THANKS

crawled along. Some of the boys toasted the crowd with bottles of champagne the first of many drinks that the team would be enjoying that day. It was a cold day, but still the crowds lined the route patiently waiting to catch a glimpse of the men. London was brought to a standstill. Crowds erupted as the bus drove past, they relished seeing the players in the flesh. For their part the players fully acknowledged and showed appreciation towards the supporters.

Opportunist shops took advantage of proceedings by selling St George flags and banners. Ordinary Christmas shoppers added to the general melee and their increased presence ensured that department store tills remained ringing. There were also numerous young, and not so young, girls waving banners with declarations of love and marriage for the handsome number 10. There was wave after wave of red and white.

It was a far cry from the celebrations thrown for the 1966 World Cup soccer stars. In a much more low-key event, Geoff Hurst and his men travelled down the Edgware Road to Kensington's Royal Garden Hotel. They were greeted by the then prime minister Harold Wilson, before tucking into a few rounds of sandwiches and beer. That

A NATION GIVES THANKS

was not the only difference between the 1966 gang and their 2003 counterparts. The footballers received a bonus of £1,000 for winning the cup whilst each man in Johnson's squad collected an extra £45,000 for their victory.

Chants of *Swing Low Sweet Chariot* reverberated around as the buses came into view. The sheer number of fans that had turned out to see them shocked both the players and staff. Some of the players were just trying to take in the atmosphere while others were speaking animatedly to friends on mobile phones or taking pictures of their fans taking pictures of them. Among the more famous supporters was former prime minister John Major, who gave them a cheery wave as they sailed passed. As well-wishers clung on high above the city's streets, Wilkinson looked uneasy. He has admitted to suffering from vertigo. After the parade he told readers of his column in *The Times* that he felt concerned for the many people he witnessed clinging onto ledges and hanging out of windows. Wilkinson doesn't know from where his fear of heights stems. He is scared that if he is ever on a high vantage point he will just run and jump off the end to see what would happen and see what it was like.

A NATION GIVES THANKS

The procession passed the Pall Mall Restaurant, in Regent Street, where the Rugby Union Football Club was formed on 26 January 1871. This was nearly 50 years after William Webb Ellis invented the game. Legend has it that in 1823 Ellis was playing football at Rugby School in Warwickshire, when he suddenly decided to pick up the ball and run with it. The pesky kid. However, instead of being sent off to do extra Latin prep or face detention, everyone played along with the 16-year-old boy. The meeting at the Pall Mall Restaurant 48 years later formed the governing body and helped tone down the slightly more violent aspects of the school's game.

An increase in decibels heralded the long-awaited arrival of the England Team on to Trafalgar Square's North Terrace. Looking out across the Square, there was a sea of red and white, flags, T-shirts and painted faces all added to the carnival feel. Two huge video screens allowed the assembled masses to chart the team's progress. The two-mile journey had taken over an hour to complete. BBC sports presenter John Inverdale greeted the players and interviewed some of them, including Clive Woodward who was stunned by the sheer size of the crowd and their enthusiastic reception. Captain Martin Johnson shared his sentiments and the hero of the hour Wilkinson added: "We're overwhelmed. It matters so much to get this support and being on this bus now is one of the greatest moments of my life." Wilkinson appeared more than a little uneasy with the rock star adulation he received even before he had a chance to utter a word. When chants of "Jonny! Jonny! Jonny!" rang out, the fly half looked as though he wouldn't mind if the ground opened up and swallowed him whole. London Mayor Ken Livingston also paid tribute to the teams' endeavours before awarding them the Freedom of the City of Greater London. This is the cue for more dry ice and the UB40 rendition of *Swing Low Sweet Chariot* to be blasted across the square. It was a day to celebrate England and a day to salute our English players.

From Trafalgar Square the team made the short journey up The Mall to Buckingham Palace for afternoon tea with the Queen. Her Royal Highness, a keen rugby fan, had managed to watch every game in the campaign except for the French clash. The team had received a good will fax from the Queen in addition to ones from Prime Minister Tony Blair. She sent a text to her

A NATION GIVES THANKS

grandson Prince Harry after the final, having listened to the match on the radio. She watched the video later. It was at her personal instigation that the team was formally invited to the Palace. The team also met the Princess Royal, another keen supporter and patron of Scottish Rugby Union, Prince Edward and Prince William. The squad had met Prince William a couple of times before when he visited them in their Twickenham changing rooms. On this occasion his familiar face and congenial manner helped them relax in these slightly more salubrious palatial surroundings. One of the biggest revelations of the whole event was the idea that the Queen can, let alone does, communicate with her grandsons via mobile text messages. No doubt signing off HRH.

The Captain of England, Martin Johnson towered over the Queen of England. The 6'7" giant had to crane his neck in order to speak to her. "So, what do you do?" was not one of the questions that the monarch had to ask when she was formally introduced to Wilkinson. The team settled down for the group photograph in the Blue Room as the Queen's corgis ran in and out of their legs. It was a somewhat surreal event by anyone's standards. The boys couldn't hang around for too long though, because they had another pressing engagement. Downing their last mouthfuls of Earl Grey, the lads hotfooted it to Number 10 Downing Street for a champagne reception.

There was already a mild controversy surrounding this event even before the team arrived. As is generally the case with government receptions, the leaders of the opposition parties were not officially invited. The Conservatives and Liberal Democrats voiced concerns that the Labour Party would bask in the glory of the victorious team and use it for political gain. A minor political skirmish was narrowly averted when the Prime Minister openly declared that he would be happy for both of the opposition leaders to attend. As it was Tony and Cherie Blair took great delight in welcoming 120 of the England entourage to their SW1 residence. This included all of the trainers and management in addition to their wives and girlfriends. Michael Howard MP and Charles Kennedy MP were also warmly welcomed. Four hundred London school children were also on hand to greet the players. The lucky pupils had been selected from 30 specialist sports colleges, and no, they weren't bunking off lessons. Wilkinson spoke to the Prime Minister about

A NATION GIVES THANKS

dealing with fame and press intrusion among other topics. Being on the receiving end of such interest, Tony Blair passed on his thoughts.

Everyone had been clambering to meet the dream team that day, ministers, monarchs and fans. It had been an amazing day for them and the country as a whole. However, the evening wasn't over yet. There was one last engagement in the packed diary. That was to be the Lawrence Dallaglio testimonial dinner, and most of the players left Downing Street to head off for the special supper. They were in for a very long night, along with some sore and fragile heads the following morning. Wilkinson had other things on his mind. The conscientious fly half was anxious to return up north to get some kicking practice in ahead of his match for Falcons that weekend.

As a result, he chose to forsake the testimonial dinner and was driven back to his home in the early hours of the morning. Whilst his car was travelling along the A1 passing through Leeming Bar Services near Catterick, it hit a patch of ice. The area is a notorious accident black spot and it was a freezing cold night. The Lexus LS430 skidded off the road and crashed into a tree, the tree was chopped in half by the impact. Had the car not been stopped by the tree undoubtedly it would have careered into the nearby 10-foot ditch. Neither Wilkinson, who was in the back chatting on his phone at the time, nor his chauffeur was hurt. A passing motorist called the police. The car had left a 40-metre skid mark on the road. Neither shaken nor stirred, Wilkinson was picked up from the minor accident site by his dad, while the chauffeur dealt with the car. Malcolm Goodwin, the driver, was in fact the owner of the executive car company that had been hired to collect Wilkinson. Goodwin had personally elected to drive the rugby star the 300-mile journey himself. Wilkinson later gave praise to his driver's skill for what could easily have been a much more serious incident. Such is the interest in all things Wilkinson, that the Surrey Toyota garage where the £56,000 car was being repaired was bombarded by calls the following day. As for Wilkinson he was back home by 3:00am and back on the pitch training seven hours later.

11

It's an honour

JONNY WILKINSON

IT'S AN HONOUR

O n 10 December, just two days after the historic London parade, Jonny was on his way back to the capital again. On this occasion he made the journey down south with his parents. Philippa and Phil were accompanying their son to Buckingham Palace for his investiture. Jonny Wilkinson's girlfriend Diana Stewart also joined the family for this special occasion. Always eager to play down his own importance, Wilkinson had to be persuaded to take his chauffeur-driven car through the Palace's VIP entrance. He would probably have been more comfortable arriving on foot and slipping in a back entrance unnoticed. As

IT'S AN HONOUR

it was, however, his silver limo swept through the grand gates and Wilkinson reflected on the fact that it was the second time he'd been here in as many days.

Dressed in a black morning jacket and lightly tanned waistcoat Wilkinson also sported a black top hat. Wilkinson had been awarded an MBE (Member of the Order of the Empire) several months before the World Cup tournament. It was purely coincidence that he was collecting the award during such a momentous week. The medal was issued in recognition of his dedication and services to rugby union. Everything Wilkinson did that week received wall-to-wall coverage. His accident hadn't managed to escape the Queen either. When he was summoned to receive his investiture, Her Royal Highness asked him about his car crash. He assured her that he was fine allaying her concerns and playing down the incident. The Queen also said how much she had enjoyed receiving the players on Monday. The two chatted for a relatively long time, after which the newly appointed Jonny Wilkinson MBE bowed and retreated. Wilkinson's parents and girlfriend all smiled broadly. At 24 Wilkinson was the youngest-ever rugby player to be awarded the honour.

JONNY WILKINSON

IT'S AN HONOUR

After the ceremony Wilkinson posed for the obligatory photographs with his new gong and his family. The pride was clearly visible on Mr and Mrs Wilkinson's faces. It had only been two weeks since Jonny's fellow sports star and friend David Beckham had been to the palace to receive his OBE, Wilkinson had texted him a congratulatory message. A lot had happened to the spirited fly half in a very short space of time, and the last few days really had been a bit of a daze – everything was going to take a while to sink in. However this was not the time to take it all in or even celebrate his most recent successes. Jonny had a plane to catch, and was whisked to the airport for the flight back to Newcastle. He told Palace reporters that he would have to celebrate his MBE in the airport lounge while waiting for his flight. As far as Wilkinson was concerned he wanted to get back to doing what he does best, playing rugby.

Sadly for Wilkinson and his fans the sprightly number 10 sustained an injury during his World Cup campaign. Not realising the extent of the injury, Wilkinson had been playing through the pain. Injuries are part of a professional rugby player's stock and trade. Wilkinson had only ever missed one England game owing to injuries

IT'S AN HONOUR

throughout his career. He has suffered consistent neck pain since he was 16-years-old and performed a particularly hard tackle while playing for Hampshire. One of the finest exponents of the art, Wilkinson routinely takes out opponents who belittle his own 13 stone. He 'hits' well over his weight, and never runs scared. He sees each tackle as a personal challenge and takes special pride in taking out guys much bigger then him. He loves watching his hardest hits on video. The secret to his deadly and devastatingly success is down to technique and timing. He had been told to sit things out on the sideline while his injury healed, and although Wilkinson was not used to life on the touchline, he was still able to do some light training to keep him occupied.

Wilkinson who had no interest and no intention of living off his last game, no matter how important, he wanted to put the past behind him and look forward to the next game. Wilkinson hadn't even watched a video of the World Cup at this stage and had no desire to. He had been there, experienced it, lived through it, but he was going to be in for a shock if he thought the public had had their fill of Wilkinson mania. In the meantime Wilkinson had more accolades to collect, he had

IT'S AN HONOUR

been honoured officially by the establishment and now it was time for the British public to bestow their highest sporting honour.

The England Rugby team were reunited once again at BBC television for another award ceremony. As Wilkinson's chauffeur-driven car swept him and his parents into the White City studios, passing a group of fans cheering his arrival, Wilkinson was still not entirely comfortable about receiving adoration but he had begun to accept and realise that there was absolutely nothing he could do about it. He greeted them with an appreciative smile and wave. The full World-Cup-winning squad was there including head coach Clive Woodward. The occasion, BBC Sports Personality of the Year 2003, attracted the cream of sportsmen and women from a variety of disciplines and the England squad took their rightful place. Wilkinson had been an avid fan of the programme and used to watch it as a child along with his family, but had never dreamed that one day he would be there himself. It was to be another one of many recent surreal occurrences in the 24-year-old's life. He was pleased that his parents were also able the share the excitement.

It was a not too surprising win for English

IT'S AN HONOUR

Rugby that night, the public wanted to thank its World Cup heroes and acknowledge their place in English history. The team were to sweep the board that night. Clive Woodward won best coach, his squad won best team and his star player, widely thought to be the best rugby union player in the world, was presented with the title BBC Sports Personality of the Year. The Princess Royal, by now a familiar friendly face to Wilkinson, presented him with the prestigious award. He was clearly nervous and the Princess was anxious to ensure that his usually safe pair of hands had a firm grip on the trophy. Wilkinson seemed to be the only one in the country that was genuinely surprised to have won. Just about everyone else in the nation had thought it was a foregone conclusion. Wilkinson received a standing ovation but was keen to share his spoils with the team at large. He also admitted to being star-struck by seeing one of his all-time heroes, tennis ace Boris Becker, in the audience. So when Becker approached the young star to congratulate him, Wilkinson could hardly contain his excitement. He was able to appreciate what it was like for his own fans when they met him for the first time. Jonny Wilkinson was the 50th holder of the BBC title and the significance

IT'S AN HONOUR

of the occasion did not pass him by, especially when he was introduced to some of the 1966 football World Cup winning team.

Not everyone was happy with the way the event had been staged. The England rugby team was presented with its trophy by ex-Australian rugby star David Campese. During his time in the Eighties and Nineties, he was England's nemesis running in many a try and slating the northern hemisphere's style of play. If was thought that having the Aussie critic present the trophy would be a way for him to publicly eat humble pie. Clive Woodward felt it was an error of judgement for Campese to grudgingly hand over an award to a team he had little respect for. Woodward thought that it would have been more appropriate for the BBC to have allowed a more respectful sportsperson to present the honour. However, David Campese had walked down Oxford Street the same week wearing a sandwich board admitting that the best team had won.

Wilkinson added the BBC award to his professional accolades. Wilkinson was named International Rugby Board's Player of the Year in addition to the Rugby Association appointing him Domestic Player of the Year. His efforts had been

IT'S AN HONOUR

recognised by Queen, country and peers alike. It was now official, Wilkinson really was as good as it gets. His sideboard was straining under the weight.

Wilkinson was looking forward to returning to the pitch at Kingston Park. His club were also looking forward to its star player's return. The tickets were impossible to get hold of for the Falcons' first match after Christmas and the club were eager to capitalise on their new-found popularity. Extra police were also drafted in to deal with the much larger than usual crowds expected. It was a good time for Wilkinson – his father and his agent had made sure that Wilkinson had only attended a few important events and that nothing had interfered with the rugby. He reportedly even managed to get one hour's worth of kicking practice in on Christmas Day. He was feeling confident and was itching to draw a line under the World Cup and move on with his career. This was to be the first step in this process.

12

Not quite business as usual

JONNY WILKINSON

NOT QUITE BUSINESS AS USUAL

Expectations were high for the Falcons game against the Northumberland Saints. Ten thousand fans packed into the Kingston Park Stadium braving a bitterly cold late December Sunday afternoon. An important game not just for Wilkinson, but also for the club as a whole, this match was part of the prized Zurich Premiership. Wilkinson received a by now familiar reception from both teams' supporters when he ran out on to the pitch with his fellow players. Things started well for the Falcons, securing an early lead within 17 minutes from kick off. Wilkinson looked confident and relaxed,

JONNY WILKINSON

NOT QUITE BUSINESS AS USUAL

He was back doing what he enjoys the most, not answering questions, not standing around in television studios, but just simply playing the game he loves. This was Wilkinson's 99th game in the Premiership and he didn't want to let anybody down. Little fear of that, because by the time the half-time whistle was blown, Wilkinson's left foot had given the team a 9-6 lead. Wilkinson's tireless training routine during the festive period had paid off.

Thirteen minutes in to the second half, Wilkinson with his customary commitment put a crunching tackle into Northampton Saints and former All Black Bruce Reihana. Wilkinson collapsed in a heap, with excruciating pain in his neck and shoulder. He knew that he had done some serious damage. It was quite literally a crushing blow for Wilkinson who was reluctantly forced to leave the field. This was certainly not the start anybody wanted to witness. Wilkinson's shoulder and neck were x-rayed that evening but, at that stage, the full extent of the damage wasn't realised. It was thought that he had just sustained soft tissue damage. But a bone split had damaged his nerves, which if not treated could leave him permanently injured.

JONNY WILKINSON

NOT QUITE BUSINESS AS USUAL

Wilkinson started his 2004, a little uncertain about his future. However, the fact that England rugby's number one was out of action made absolutely no difference to his popularity. He was recognised in the Queen's New Years Honours list, being awarded an OBE in light of his World Cup success, only a few months after collecting his MBE. The rugby star was also immortalised in wax at Madame Tussauds in London. His waxwork was sculptured using photographs and video clips in an effort to achieve an accurate representation. The interactive exhibit shows Jonny dressed in his full England kit and adopting his trademark pre-kick stance. It encourages visitors to 'Do The Jonny' by practising their own kicking skills next to the master.

The New Year also saw the English hero immortalised in verse. Poet Laureate Andrew Motion was so moved by the fly half's World Cup performance that he was forced to put pen to paper. The composition took four months to complete because Motion found it extremely difficult to find anything that would rhyme with 'Wilkinson'. In the end he opted to come up with the slightly easier option of finding words that rhymed with 'Jonny'.

JONNY WILKINSON

NOT QUITE BUSINESS AS USUAL

Wilkinson's wildfire popularity was not confined to the UK. Jonny Wilkinson is going to have a Spanish road named after him. The local government in Calvia, Majorca have authorised the naming ceremony, which is scheduled to take place this summer during the course of the Rugby Seven's tournament. It is thought that the final name will be either, Carrer or Avinguda Jonny Wilkinson. Wilkinson and his family are regular visitors to Majorca, a region that they love.

Although keeping busy off the pitch with fitness and kicking practice, Wilkinson had spent less then an hour playing match rugby since his momentous World Cup victory. Wilkinson was understandably upset, and although he put a brave face on things, underneath it all he must have been desperately frustrated. Anyone who knows the man knows he lives for rugby and not being allowed to play the game he loves would always be a devastating blow. After consultations with surgeons they eventually decided that an operation was called for, so in February 2004 Wilkinson went under the knife.

Wilkinson was in for the waiting game, he had to do something he wasn't used to, he had to take things slowly. Wilkinson's injury is taking its time

NOT QUITE BUSINESS AS USUAL

to heal but he has come to terms with the fact that it's a slow process and that he has to be patient.

In April, Wilkinson was invited to do some more TV work, it was an interview request. Ordinarily Wilkinson would have dismissed the offer, but this was a request from the daddy of all talk show hosts. Michael Parkinson had put in a bid to chat with England's first son, and Wilkinson couldn't turn him down. Like most of the nation Wilkinson grew up watching Michael Parkinson on TV and was flattered to be invited as a guest on what was to be one of the Parkinson's last chat shows for the BBC. This was Wilkinson's first full TV interview since the World Cup victory. It was to be another proud night for Wilkinson and his family.

Wilkinson descended the Parkinson staircase to the sound of *Swing Low Sweet Chariot*, which was being belted out by the live studio orchestra. He received a standing ovation, this was the first time that Michael Parkinson could ever recall this happening to a guest. Dressed in a dark suit and striped open-necked shirt, Wilkinson looked happy and relaxed. During the 20-minute chat Wilkinson discussed his feelings after he scored the winning drop goal and how he had come to understand his own celebrity among other issues. 'That kick' was

NOT QUITE BUSINESS AS USUAL

also given a screening to rapturous applause. Parkinson probed the rugby star about his sex symbol status. Reluctantly the England hero acknowledged that he had a large female following, but in a typically self-deprecating manner stated that he only seemed to appeal to "Girls under 11 and over 60!".

The England star was also asked to lend his services to the Flora London Marathon. He started the 26.2-mile event alongside the record-breaking runner, Sir Roger Bannister. The 33,000 runners were confronted by an overcast and gloomy Sunday morning, but their spirits remained high throughout. Jonny Wilkinson could really relate to the standard of commitment and training that was needed to take part in, let alone complete, the marathon. He was full of admiration, especially for the fun runners who raised huge amounts of cash for their charities. Sporting celebrities, ex-cricketer Graham Gooch and former England football manager Graham Taylor were among those being cheered on by Wilkinson and the half-a-million-strong crowd.

13

The future

THE FUTURE

T here's no doubt that the events in Telstra Stadium last November did a lot for English rugby, but it also did a great deal to boost the nation as a whole. Rugby has always been an underdog to its much more popular and lucrative soccer cousin. However, the historic win benefited all British sports. English supremacy on the sporting stage bolsters sport and sportsmen at all levels. Success encourages investment; investment allows development, which in turn encourages success. The fact that the majority of people that turned out to welcome the World Cup winning team were not rugby fans really didn't matter.

THE FUTURE

They were able to enjoy and celebrate an all-too-rare English World Cup victory. Hopefully some of those supporters will retain an interest in the sport and even go to a few games. Rugby Union is an all-encompassing sport, it has always attracted a diverse crowd. Luckily the sport has never been blighted by the hooliganism that football has had to endure over the years. However, the governing bodies of the sport need to build on this initial success and look to the future, so that this victory doesn't remain a one-off. The new Jonny Wilkinsons must have the support and nurturing they require at an early age, so that they can develop into world-class players. Ambition and dedication is a given, but the support mechanisms must be in place to move the new players forward. Many schools have adopted rugby in light of the recent international success, and these initiatives are required if England is to be regularly represented on the winning rostrum.

At present, the golden boy Wilkinson is dealing with his own personal setback, he is biding his time. Wilkinson could do irreversible damage to himself if he were to come back to the game before his shoulder has fully healed. He realises that, but it doesn't really make things

THE FUTURE

much easier for him. He is the eternal optimist – his glass is always half full. What helps Wilkinson is his belief in himself, the commitment he has to the sport, and the support of his family and teammates both Falcon and England. He is still very much part of the Newcastle Falcons family, and indeed Newcastle as a whole. This was reinforced when he was recently awarded the Honourary Freedom of the City of Newcastle upon Tyne. He was the 85th recipient of the award, which has also been given to Newcastle United striker Alan Shearer and former South African president Nelson Mandela among others. Wilkinson continues to motivate other players sharing the team's highs and lows. He trains up to three times a day with his specialist coaches and when he does come back he will be fitter and stronger than ever before. At 24-years-old, Wilkinson is still very young in terms of development and experts in the field generally believe that the fly half won't reach his full potential until he is in his late 20s. However, long before then a new, even better Jonny Wilkinson will emerge, his unyielding dedication and the sheer bloody-mindedness that has driven him thus far is still burning deep within. Far from being despondent

THE FUTURE

he has set himself new career goals, in the same way he did when he was eleven. No one doubts that he'll achieve his new professional ambitions.

Today Wilkinson can still be seen practising his kicking late into the evening under the floodlights at Kingston Park. His endless, almost obsessive pursuit of excellence is still unrelenting. Some things never change. Long after his colleagues have departed, his solitary figure is out on the training park. "Just a couple more kicks," he says to himself, before adopting that trademark stance.

14

The fun, bluffer's guide to the England team and rugby union

JONNY WILKINSON

THE ENGLAND TEAM

Trevor Woodman MBE is the first man in this line up. He wears the number one shirt and plays as a Loosehead prop. He is one of three men at the front of the scrum. These are tough guys usually quite bulky they also have a tremendous degree of strength. Woodman at 6' is relatively tall for this position. The players who partake in the scrums are called forwards. The Loosehead prop stands on the hookers left side.

The hooker, no not a lady of the night, so when one's quite finished sniggering... The hooker gets his name from the fact that he uses his foot to hook the ball back when it is put into the scrum. *Steve Thompson MBE* did this job very successfully for the England World Cup team. He has fast reaction times and ensures that the ball was heading out of the scrum almost as soon as it was put in. He is propped up in between the two props standing either side of him. The other job of the hooker is to throw the ball for lineouts. It's important that they are accurate throwers thereby giving their teammates a good chance of jumping up and catching the ball.

The third and last man in the front row is the

tighthead prop. He stands on the right hand side of the Hooker. *Phil Vickery MBE* fulfiled this role in Telstra Stadium. At over 6' and 19st Vickery was able to use his considerable upper body strength to good effect driving back the Australians.

'Colossal Captain' *Martin Johnson OBE* plays at Second Row, tucked in behind the props and hooker. At six foot six and weighing in at over 18st he is called Johno by teammates, but with his imposing presence everyone else is more likely to address him as 'Sir'. The Second Row are invariably tall, they are the ones who tend to win the ball from a lineout. They have to be powerhouses as well with very strong legs so that they can drive the scrum forward. He does the job extremely effectively and has picked up 77 caps during his career. Very much respected by his players, this captain likes to lead by example, in his eyes actions speak louder then words. Johno's partner in crime is *Ben Kay MBE*. The 29-nine-year old is the same height as his captain, though at 17st 9lbs he is a bit lighter. Second Rows often wear head guards or binding in an effort to protect their ears when they scrum down, but even so cauliflower ears tend to be the end result of any hard played career.

JONNY WILKINSON

THE ENGLAND TEAM

Richard Hill MBE playing at blindside flanker, has all the required attributes he's fast and fit. Hill binds in around Martin Johnson on the captain's left hand side, he's directly behind Trevor Woodman. The other flanker is called the Openside Flanker. *Neil Back MBE* takes care of things in this position and has clocked up 66 caps doing just that. He has to get stuck into a lot of tackling. Ironically and somewhat confusingly Back is not a back at all, being part of the eight-man scrum, he's a forward. The flankers also have an important role in the lineout and are often also targeted by their hookers. Flankers are also called upon to put pressure on the opposition's fly half, preventing them from scoring winning drop goals, or gaining ground.

The Number Eight is the eighth and last man in the scrum. Most appropriately he wears the number eight on his back, no not Neil Back he wears number seven. Anyway, *Lawrence Bruno Nero Dallaglio MBE* plays this position for England. His teammates refer to him as 'Lol' because by the time they have called out his full name the match is generally over. Dallaglio combines the power of a forward with a good turn of speed. It takes a very brave man to stop the 6' 4" 17stoner when he's running at full pelt.

The scrum half has a huge responsibility resting on his broad shoulders. Luckily for England they had *Matt Dawson MBE* taking up the challenge in Australia. It was his job to get the ball from the forwards in the scrum and pass it out to a back. Dawson was always on his toes looking out for potential threats and opportunities to set up his player whenever there is space. The scrum half need to be able to read the game well and can dictate the speed and direction of play. He plays alongside his full half colleague.

The most famous and talented number 10 in the world is *Jonny Wilkinson OBE*. Wilko plays in the Fly Half position, the skills that he has mastered hold true for every Fly Half. They have to be good kickers but they also have to be cool under pressure, this is especially useful when kicking the winning points in the rugby world cup final. It also helps if they are ferocious tacklers because they will be given plenty of opportunities to display this ability. As a back, the player will also be one of the more handsome men on the pitch. Backs tend to be

THE ENGLAND TEAM

the players most likely to be offered lucrative modelling contracts during or after their professional rugby careers.

Ben Cohen MBE supplies one of the two winger's duties in the England squad he share the responsibility with 'Billy Whiz', *Jason Robinson MBE*. These two are the fastest men on the England team. Robinson scored the only English try in the world cup final. However as well as being lightening quick sprinters they also have to be robust enough to take and dish out hefty tackles. The main role is to find space on the pitch so that they can run in the tries. Wingers will often have a high points ratio and heaps of glory levelled at him.

The Inside Centre players a major role in defence, they have to be excellent passers of the ball in addition to fast runners. *Mike Tindall MBE* executes this job superbly. Tindall often has to draw opposition players in to him before off loading the ball to a waiting winger. The 6'3" *Will Greenwood MBE* played as Outside Centre with Tindall in Australia. Both men kept an eye out for any beckoning breaks in the Wallabies defensive

THE ENGLAND TEAM

wall and broke through whenever the slightest of gaps presented themselves.

Wearing the number 15 jersey for England's last match in Australia was *Josh Lewsey MBE*. He is the Full Back and represent's the team's last line of defence. If the opposition do manage to blitz through the other 14 players all eyes look towards the full back to spare their blushes. Like Lewsey all full-backs should also be exemplary catchers of the ball. They must be able to judge a ball's height and distance precisely so that they can make a clean catch. They often have to hold their ground even though they know that opposition players will be crashing into them at any moment. Being able to keep their nerve is one of their most important features. They also have to be able to 'dispose' of the ball, by kicking, running, passing in fact anything that will clear the immediate danger.

JONNY WILKINSON

A ROUGH GUIDE TO RUGBY UNION

Basic principles of the game:
Like so many other sports the whole point of rugby union is to win. It's quite simple. One team has to score more points then the other. There are a variety of ways by which this can be achieved. Putting the ball down on or over the goal line secures a try that is worth five points. The try can then be converted. This is done by kicking the ball through the upright posts and over the cross bar. A successful conversion will result in two more points. Points can also be gained from penalties by kicking the ball through the upright posts. This is worth three points. Another three-point option is the drop goal. The ball must hit the ground before it's given a hefty whack between the posts. Rather like football, the game starts with a kick off but unlike football each half lasts 40 minutes and each team has fifteen players. There's also the question of the ball, because of its shape, it's bounce is therefore very unpredictable.

Formation of the scrum:
This consists of eight players from each team locked together driving forward, pushing their opponent's back. Each team has eight men in the scrum – they are all forwards and sometimes

referred to as the pack. The hooker uses his feet to hook the ball back to his number eight. Either side of the hooker are the props. Behind them are the second row plus two flankers one on each side. There is a number eight at the back. He can control the ball with his feet until the scrum half is ready for it. It is a 3,4,1 formation. Scrums are formed when the ball is knocked on, passed forward or if there is some form of non-serious infringement. The scrum half puts the ball into the scrum, he waits until the ball is hooked or tapped out by a number eight's boot before he grabs the ball. No one handles the ball until it has left the scrum. The number eight will sometimes retain the ball within the confines of the scrum while his team go forward in an effort to gain ground. Once the ball has left the scrum the opposition scrum half will usually make a play for the ball and the scrum will disband.

The lineout:
When the ball goes out of play into the sidelines a lineout is awarded. Similar to a football throw-in, whichever team didn't put the ball to go into touch is allowed to throw the ball back into play. That is unless the team that kicked it out and did so as a

result of a penalty. In that case they will be the ones to throw the ball back into the lineout. Whichever team was awarded the throw-in, dictates the number of players in the line. The opposition team must match the number of players whether there are all eight forwards plus the scrum involved or just a couple. It's even possible to throw the ball yourself if you're very flash. Both the ball and the players must be in a straight line. There has to be one metre between the teams. Players lift one another up to catch the ball once the ball leaves the hookers' hands. The successful player will either catch the ball or tap it back to his side in order that it can be passed out to the backs. If the ball is not thrown straight or there is an infringe-ment, for example, one team interferes with the other, they will be penalised. The other team will be given the choice of retaking the lineout or having a scrum. In each instant it will be the team that has been infringed that will have the throw or put in.

Rucks and mauls:
These sound rough and they can be. A ruck ensues when the ball is on the ground and there is at least one player from either side struggling over it. Other plays can join in they must remain on their

feet in order to handle the ball and they must join in the action from behind the ball they cannot enter from the side. A maul requires three players from each side challenging each other for the ball. One of the teams will have the ball in their possession not in the ground but safely cosseted in one of the player's hands. The players must bind together and if the play does eventually break down without one or other side gaining possession and getting the ball out, the team that is driving forward will be awarded the scrum.

The tackle:
Not a reference to fishing equipment or indeed anything else. The tackle is an integral part of the game. It is often referred to as a hit although there is no hitting involved or at least there shouldn't be. When a player is tackled this can result in a maul if the tackled player remains on his feet and other players come in to support. However if the player is tackled and brought down to the ground then he must release the ball. It is against the rules for players to handle the ball whilst on the ground. It is also against the rules and very dangerous to perform a high tackle, that is aiming at the opponent's throat or head. Some

of the best tacklers aim at their opposition's legs or waist. It is also against the rules to tackle a player when they don't have one foot on the ground i.e. when they're jumping.

Passing/knock on:

In rugby union the ball must be passed backwards, any infringement will be punished with a scrum awarded against them. If the ball goes forward even accidentally it is called a knock on and again will be punished. It is possible however, to kick the ball ahead which can then be chased by fellow players.

Sin bin:

Naughty players are sent to the sin bin if the referee deems that their offense is serious enough to be shown the yellow card. The player will spend 10 minutes in the sin bin in which time they will be able to reflect on their wrong-doings. Meanwhile, their teammates will have to play on without them. As in football, players are sent off completely for serious offences.

Blood bin:

Not an actual place, this term is used when a player

has to leave the field of play for treatment to a bleeding wound. Whilst the injured player is off getting stitched, a 'blood replacement' takes his place until he is fit to return.

Bath:

This really is best to be avoided. Sharing a large bathtub with 14 other blokes can never be encouraged and this is no exception.

Bar:

Not the crossbar, the drink's bar. This is one of the most important places in rugby, since the game turned professional in 1995 player's attitudes to alcohol have had to change a little bit. However, the bar is still very much part of the rugby supporter's agenda and it is likely to remain that way for the foreseeable future.

BIOGRAPHIES

OTHER BOOKS IN THE SERIES

Also available in the series:

OTHER BOOKS IN THE SERIES

JENNIFER ANISTON

She's been a Friend to countless millions worldwide, and overcame numerous hurdles to rise to the very top of her field. From a shy girl with a dream of being a famous actress, through being reduced to painting scenery for high school plays, appearing in a series of flop TV shows and one rather bad movie, Jennifer Aniston has persevered, finally finding success at the very top of the TV tree.

Bringing the same determination that got her a part on the world's best-loved TV series to her attempts at a film career, she's also worked her way from rom-com cutie up to serious, respected actress and box office draw, intelligently combining indie, cult and comedy movies into a blossoming career which looks set to shoot her to the heights of Hollywood's A-list. She's also found love with one of the world's most desirable men. Is Jennifer Aniston the ultimate Hollywood Renaissance woman? It would seem she's got more than a shot at such a title, as indeed, she seems to have it all, even if things weren't always that way. Learn all about Aniston's rise to fame in this compelling biography.

OTHER BOOKS IN THE SERIES

DAVID BECKHAM

This book covers the amazing life of the boy from East London who has not only become a world class footballer and the captain of England, but also an idol to millions, and probably the most famous man in Britain.

His biography tracks his journey, from the playing fields of Chingford to the Bernabau. It examines how he joined his beloved Manchester United and became part of a golden generation of talent that led to United winning trophies galore.

Beckham's parallel personal life is also examined, as he moved from tongue-tied football-obsessed kid to suitor of a Spice Girl, to one half of Posh & Becks, the most famous celebrity couple in Britain – perhaps the world. His non-footballing activities, his personal indulgences and changing styles have invited criticism, and even abuse, but his football talent has confounded the critics, again and again.

The biography looks at his rise to fame and his relationship with Posh, as well as his decision to leave Manchester for Madrid. Has it affected his relationship with Posh? What will the latest controversy over his sex life mean for celebrity's royal couple? And will he come back to play in England again?

OTHER BOOKS IN THE SERIES

GEORGE CLOONEY

The tale of George Clooney's astonishing career is an epic every bit as riveting as one of his blockbuster movies. It's a story of tenacity and determination, of fame and infamy, a story of succeeding on your own terms regardless of the risks. It's also a story of emergency rooms, batsuits, tidal waves and killer tomatoes, but let's not get ahead of ourselves.

Born into a family that, by Sixties' Kentucky standards, was dripping with show business glamour, George grew up seeing the hard work and heartache that accompanied a life in the media spotlight.

By the time stardom came knocking for George Clooney, it found a level-headed and mature actor ready and willing to embrace the limelight, while still indulging a lifelong love of partying and practical jokes. A staunchly loyal friend and son, a bachelor with a taste for the high life, a vocal activist for the things he believes and a born and bred gentleman; through failed sitcoms and blockbuster disasters, through artistic credibility and box office success, George Clooney has remained all of these things...and much, much more. Prepare to meet Hollywood's most fascinating megastar in this riveting biography.

BILLY CONNOLLY

In a 2003 London Comedy Poll to find Britain's favourite comedian, Billy Connolly came out on top. It's more than just Billy Connolly's all-round comic genius that puts him head and shoulders above the rest. Connolly has also proved himself to be an accomplished actor with dozens of small and big screen roles to his name. In 2003, he could be seen in *The Last Samurai* with Tom Cruise.

Connolly has also cut the mustard in the USA, 'breaking' that market in a way that chart-topping pop groups since The Beatles and the Stones have invariably failed to do, let alone mere stand-up comedians. Of course, like The Beatles and the Stones, Billy Connolly has been to the top of the pop charts too with D.I.V.O.R.C.E. in 1975.

On the way he's experienced heartache of his own with a difficult childhood and a divorce of his own, found the time and energy to bring up five children, been hounded by the press on more than one occasion, and faced up to some considerable inner demons. But Billy Connolly is a survivor. Now in his 60s, he's been in show business for all of 40 years, and 2004 finds him still touring. This exciting biography tells the story an extraordinary entertainer.

OTHER BOOKS IN THE SERIES

ROBERT DE NIRO

Robert De Niro is cinema's greatest chameleon. Snarling one minute, smirking the next, he's straddled Hollywood for a quarter of a century, making his name as a serious character actor, in roles ranging from psychotic taxi drivers to hardened mobsters. The scowls and pent-up violence may have won De Niro early acclaim but, ingeniously, he's now playing them for laughs, poking fun at the tough guy image he so carefully cultivated. Ever the perfectionist, De Niro holds nothing back on screen, but in real life he is a very private man – he thinks of himself as just another guy doing a job. Some job, some guy. There's more to the man than just movies. De Niro helped New York pick itself up after the September 11 terrorist attacks on the Twin Towers by launching the TriBeCa Film Festival and inviting everyone downtown. He runs several top-class restaurants and has dated some of the most beautiful women in the world, least of all supermodel Naomi Campbell. Now in his 60s, showered with awards and a living legend, De Niro's still got his foot on the pedal. There are six, yes six, films coming your way in 2004. In this latest biography, you'll discover all about his latest roles and the life of this extraordinary man.

OTHER BOOKS IN THE SERIES

MICHAEL DOUGLAS

Douglas may have been a shaggy-haired member of a hippy commune in the Sixties but just like all the best laidback, free-loving beatniks, he's gone on to blaze a formidable career, in both acting and producing.

In a career that has spanned nearly 40 years so far, Douglas has produced a multitude of hit movies including the classic *One Flew Over The Cuckoo's Nest* and *The China Syndrome* through to box office smashes such as *Starman* and *Face/Off*.

His acting career has been equally successful – from *Romancing The Stone* to *Wall Street* to *Fatal Attraction*, Douglas's roles have shown that he isn't afraid of putting himself on the line when up there on the big screen.

His relationship with his father; his stay in a top clinic to combat his drinking problem; the breakdown of his first marriage; and his publicised clash with the British media have all compounded to create the image of a man who's transformed himself from being the son of Hollywood legend Kirk Douglas, into Kirk Douglas being the dad of Hollywood legend, Michael Douglas.

OTHER BOOKS IN THE SERIES

HUGH GRANT

He's the Oxford fellow who stumbled into acting, the middle-class son of a carpet salesman who became famous for bumbling around stately homes and posh weddings. The megastar actor who claims he doesn't like acting, but has appeared in over 40 movies and TV shows.

On screen he's romanced a glittering array of Hollywood's hottest actresses, and tackled medical conspiracies and the mafia. Off screen he's hogged the headlines with his high profile girlfriend as well as finding lifelong notoriety after a little Divine intervention in Los Angeles.

Hugh Grant is Britain's biggest movie star, an actor whose talent for comedy has often been misjudged by those who assume he simply plays himself.

From bit parts in Nottingham theatre, through comedy revues at the Edinburgh Fringe, and on to the top of the box office charts, Hugh has remained constant – charming, witty and ever so slightly sarcastic, obsessed with perfection and performance while winking to his audience as if to say: "This is all awfully silly, isn't it?" Don't miss this riveting biography.

OTHER BOOKS IN THE SERIES

MICHAEL JACKSON

Friday 29 August 1958 was not a special day in Gary, Indiana, and indeed Gary, was far from being a special place. But it was on this day and in this location that the world's greatest entertainer was to be born, Michael Joseph Jackson.

The impact that this boy was destined to have on the world of entertainment could never have been estimated. Here we celebrate Michael Jackson's extraordinary talents, and plot the defining events over his 40-year career. This biography explores the man behind the myth, and gives an understanding of what drives this special entertainer.

In 1993, there was an event that was to rock Jackson's world. His friendship with a 12-year-old boy and the subsequent allegations resulted in a lawsuit, a fall in record sales and a long road to recovery. Two marriages, three children and 10 years later there is a feeling of déjà vu as Jackson again deals with more controversy. Without doubt, 2004 proves to be the most important year in the singer's life. Whatever that future holds for Jackson, his past is secured, there has never been and there will never again be anything quite like Michael Jackson.

OTHER BOOKS IN THE SERIES

NICOLE KIDMAN

On 23 March 2003 Nicole Kidman won the Oscar for Best Actress for her role as Virginia Woolf in *The Hours*. That was the night that marked Nicole Kidman's acceptance into the upper echelons of Hollywood royalty. She had certainly come a long way from the 'girlfriend' roles she played when she first arrived in Hollywood – in films such as *Billy Bathgate* and *Batman Forever* – although even then she managed to inject her 'pretty girl' roles with an edge that made her acting stand out. And she was never merely content to be Mrs Cruise, movie star's wife. Although she stood dutifully behind her then husband in 1993 when he was given his star on the Hollywood Walk of Fame, Nicole got a star of her own 10 years later, in 2003.

Not only does Nicole Kidman have stunning good looks and great pulling power at the box office, she also has artistic credibility. But Nicole has earned the respect of her colleagues, working hard and turning in moving performances from a very early age. Although she dropped out of school at 16, no one doubts the intelligence and passion that are behind the fiery redhead's acting career, which includes television and stage work, as well as films. Find out how Kidman became one of Hollywood's most respected actresses in this compelling biography.

OTHER BOOKS IN THE SERIES

JENNIFER LOPEZ

There was no suggestion that the Jennifer Lopez of the early Nineties would become the accomplished actress, singer and icon that she is today. Back then she was a dancer on the popular comedy show *In Living Color* – one of the Fly Girls, the accompaniment, not the main event. In the early days she truly was Jenny from the block; the Bronx native of Puerto Rican descent – another hopeful from the east coast pursuing her dreams in the west.

Today, with two marriages under her belt, three multi-platinum selling albums behind her and an Oscar-winning hunk as one of her ex-boyfriends, she is one of the most talked about celebrities of the day. Jennifer Lopez is one of the most celebrated Hispanic actresses of all time.

Her beauty, body and famous behind, are lusted after by men and envied by women throughout the world. She has proven that she can sing, dance and act. Yet her critics dismiss her as a diva without talent. And the criticisms are not just about her work, some of them are personal. But what is the reality? Who is Jennifer Lopez, where did she come from and how did get to where she is now? This biography aims to separate fact from fiction to reveal the real Jennifer Lopez.

OTHER BOOKS IN THE SERIES

MADONNA

Everyone thought they had Madonna figured out in early 2003. The former Material Girl had become Maternal Girl, giving up on causing controversy to look after her two children and set up home in England with husband Guy Ritchie. The former wild child had settled down and become respectable. The new Madonna would not do anything to shock the establishment anymore, she'd never do something like snogging both Britney Spears and Christina Aguilera at the MTV Video Music Awards... or would she?

Of course she would. Madonna has been constantly reinventing herself since she was a child, and her ability to shock even those who think they know better is both a tribute to her business skills and the reason behind her staying power. Only Madonna could create gossip with two of the current crop of pop princesses in August and then launch a children's book in September. In fact, only Madonna would even try.

In her 20-year career she has not just been a successful pop singer, she is also a movie star, a business woman, a stage actress, an author and a mother. Find out all about this extraordinary modern-day icon in this new compelling biography.

OTHER BOOKS IN THE SERIES

BRAD PITT

From the launch pad that was his scene stealing turn in *Thelma And Louise* as the sexual-enlightening bad boy. To his character-driven performances in dramas such as *Legends of the Fall* through to his Oscar-nominated work in *Twelve Monkeys* and the dark and razor-edged Tyler Durden in *Fight Club*, Pitt has never rested on his laurels. Or his good looks.

And the fact that his love life has garnered headlines all over the world hasn't hindered Brad Pitt's profile away from the screen either – linked by the press to many women, his relationships with the likes of Juliette Lewis and Gwyneth Paltrow. Then of course, in 2000, we had the Hollywood fairytale ending when he tied the silk knot with Jennifer Aniston.

Pitt's impressive track record as a superstar, sex symbol *and* credible actor looks set to continue as he has three films lined up for release over the next year – as Achilles in the Wolfgang Peterson-helmed Troy; Rusty Ryan in the sequel *Ocean's Twelve* and the titular Mr Smith in the thriller *Mr & Mrs Smith* alongside Angelina Jolie. Pitt's ever-growing success shows no signs of abating. Discover all about Pitt's meteoric rise from rags to riches in this riveting biography.

OTHER BOOKS IN THE SERIES

SHANE RICHIE

Few would begrudge the current success of 40-year-old Shane Richie. To get where he is today, Shane has had a rather bumpy roller coaster ride that has seen the hard working son of poor Irish immigrants endure more than his fair share of highs and lows – financially, professionally and personally.

In the space of four decades he has amused audiences at school plays, realised his childhood dream of becoming a Pontins holiday camp entertainer, experienced homelessness, beat his battle with drink, became a million-aire then lost the lot. He's worked hard and played hard.

When the producers of *EastEnders* auditioned Shane for a role in the top TV soap, they decided not to give him the part, but to create a new character especially for him. That character was Alfie Moon, manager of the Queen Vic pub, and very quickly Shane's TV alter ego has become one of the most popular soap characters in Britain. This biography is the story of a boy who had big dreams and never gave up on turning those dreams into reality

OTHER BOOKS IN THE SERIES

ROBBIE WILLIAMS

Professionally, things can't get much better for Robbie Williams. In 2002 he signed the largest record deal in UK history when he re-signed with EMI. The following year he performed to over 1.5 million fans on his European tour, breaking all attendance records at Knebworth with three consecutive sell-out gigs.

Since going solo Robbie Williams has achieved five number one hit singles, five number one hit albums; 10 Brits and three Ivor Novello awards. When he left the highly successful boy band Take That in 1995 his future seemed far from rosy. He got off to a shaky start. His nemesis, Gary Barlow, had already recorded two number one singles and the press had virtually written Williams off. But then in December 1997, he released his Christmas single, *Angels.*

Angels re-launched his career – it remained in the Top 10 for 11 weeks. Since then Robbie has gone from strength to strength, both as a singer and a natural showman. His live videos are a testament to his performing talent and his promotional videos are works of art.

This biography tells of Williams' journey to the top – stopping off on the way to take a look at his songs, his videos, his shows, his relationships, his rows, his record deals and his demons.